Praise for *The Upper Hand*

"Dr. Abbie Maroño revolutionizes the way we think about persuasion, showing that true power lies not in manipulation but in building authentic connections rooted in trust and empathy. A must-read for leaders and negotiators, this book equips us to achieve our goals while uplifting others, making it essential in today's disconnected world."

—Robin Dreeke, FBI Special Agent (ret.) Spy Recruiter and Trust Expert

"*The Upper Hand* is a revolutionary guide that blends cutting-edge science with practical strategies. It offers a powerful tool kit for building trust, mastering communication, and achieving success in both personal and professional spheres."

—Joe Navarro, #1 Bestselling Author and Leading Body Language Expert

"*The Upper Hand* is a master class in trust and influence, showing the power of cooperation over coercion. Dr. Maroño provides practical tools to approach conversations with confidence, making this book a cornerstone for transforming your personal and professional life."

—Brad Beeler, Supervisory Special Agent, US Secret Service

"Dr. Abbie's *The Upper Hand* is a groundbreaking guide to ethical influence and persuasion. Rooted in the science of social engineering, it empowers readers to achieve their goals, build meaningful connections, and create desired outcomes—all without the need for manipulation."

—Judd Shaw, Speaker, Author, Attorney, and Serial Entrepreneur

"Dr. Abbie's *The Upper Hand* is an essential playbook for business professionals. This book is packed with actionable techniques that will sharpen your ability to connect, negotiate, and lead with authenticity and effectiveness. It is an indispensable guide for executives, managers, and anyone striving to lead with impact."

—Guillermo de Nicolas, Founder and CEO, Panther Capital Group

"Dr Abbie's book is a true game-changer. Packed with cutting-edge insights, practical strategies, and compelling examples, this book arms you with the tools to influence and thrive in any situation. A must-read for anyone looking to elevate their communication and negotiation skills."

—Giles Paley-Phillips, Award-Winning Author, Podcaster, and Screenwriter

"Dr. Abbie Maroño has been one of the most requested guests ever on *The Mojo Sessions*—and for good reason. Abbie has the unique ability to take the valuable research from her lab and from others around the world, and distill it in a way to help us better understand ourselves and how we interact with the world. Abbie is smart, genuine, and articulate, and her empathic nature makes it easy for us to relate to her work. *The Upper Hand* beautifully outlines the latest principles of social engineering, challenging the current constructs we use in our interactions and shows how through some clever changes, we can prosper in our negotiations and communication with others."

—Gary Bertwistle, Keynote Speaker, Author, and Host, *The Mojo Sessions* podcast

"*The Upper Hand* is a modern, science-backed guide to winning friends and influencing people. Get what you want—no leverage needed! This insightful book reveals the art of social engineering and secrets used by highly successful people, presented in a practical guide."

—Nadia Ait, Cofounder and CEO, Body Language Academy

"Dr. Abbie's new read *The Upper Hand* is not just another run of the mill book on persuasion, It is the blueprint of understanding human behavior and building trust with integrity. Packed with actionable insights, it teaches you to influence ethically, whether in your career, relationships, or everyday life. This is the book that will help you finally feel like you can now truly connect and succeed."

—Shawn Livingston, Keynote Speaker, Podcaster, and Combat Veteran

THE
UPPER
HAND

Also by Dr. Abbie Maroño

*Work in Progress: The Road to Empowerment,
the Journey Through Shame*

THE UPPER HAND

Mastering Persuasion and Getting What You Want with the Science of Social Engineering

DR. ABBIE MAROÑO

Matt Holt Books
An Imprint of BenBella Books, Inc.
Dallas, TX

The Upper Hand copyright © 2025 by Abbie Maroño

All rights reserved. Except in the case of brief quotations embodied in critical articles or reviews, no part of this book may be used or reproduced, stored, transmitted, or used in any manner whatsoever, including for training artificial intelligence (AI) technologies or for automated text and data mining, without prior written permission from the publisher.

Matt Holt is an imprint of BenBella Books, Inc.
8080 N. Central Expressway
Suite 1700
Dallas, TX 75206
benbellabooks.com
Send feedback to feedback@benbellabooks.com

BenBella and *Matt Holt* are federally registered trademarks.

Printed in the United States of America
10 9 8 7 6 5 4 3 2 1

Library of Congress Control Number: 2024057715
ISBN 9781637746844 (hardcover)
ISBN 9781637746851 (electronic)

Editing by Corrine Hickin, Virginia Combs, and Katie Dickman
Copyediting by Evan Herrington
Proofreading by Marissa Wold Uhrina and Lisa Story
Indexing by WordCo Indexing Services, Inc.
Text design and composition by Jordan Koluch
Cover design by Brigid Pearson
Printed by Lake Book Manufacturing

Special discounts for bulk sales are available.
Please contact bulkorders@benbellabooks.com.

To my father,
for being my unwavering support, my guiding strength,
and the first person I turn to, no matter what life brings.
Thank you for teaching me to pull myself out of the dirt,
get back on my feet, and never back down.
This book is for you.

Contents

Foreword   xi

Introduction   1

PART I: UNDERSTANDING INFLUENCE

Chapter 1: Wielding The Upper Hand   11
Chapter 2: The Dark Side of Social Engineering   33
Chapter 3: Overcoming Influence Misconceptions   51

PART II: USING INFLUENCE

Chapter 4: Getting a Grip on The Upper Hand   73
Chapter 5: Create a Tribe   95
Chapter 6: Speak Their Language   111

Chapter 7: Pants Yourself	133
Chapter 8: Shelve It	151
Chapter 9: Hold, Don't Squeeze	173
Chapter 10: The Prosocial Engineer	195
Acknowledgments	205
Notes	207
Index	213

Foreword

In a world where the subtle currents of human influence shape every decision we make, understanding these forces becomes both a challenge and an opportunity. *The Upper Hand* delves into the profound biological, anatomical, physiological, neurological, social, and ethological imperatives that define humanity. These elements form the foundation of our unique capacity for connection and understanding—qualities that arise from the intricate interplay of the human mind and body.

As Dr. Maroño articulates with great precision, human evolution has endowed us with DNA-driven imperatives rooted deeply in biology. This book seeks to reaffirm the unparalleled importance of human connection and what influences us. It emphasizes the irreplaceable, nuanced interactions we share face-to-face, touch-to-touch, through which we not only perpetuate our species but also cultivate friendships, foster trust, and thrive as social, sentient beings. In re-centering our focus on these foundational aspects of human life, this work reminds us of the deeply consequential role our

FOREWORD

interactions play, shaping not only individual lives but also the very fabric of society.

Dr. Maroño offers a fascinating perspective on influence and sociability, portraying social engineering as the art and science of building relationships that are mutually beneficial, ethical, and rewarding. She redefines influence not as a mysterious force, but as a skill rooted in understanding human behavior and the factors that drive connection and cooperation. By breaking down the science of why certain behaviors foster trust and mutual benefit, she illustrates how influence is more about purposeful, prosocial efforts than manipulation. This approach brings clarity to the ways we can all create meaningful connections that are not only effective but also enjoyable.

Every so often, a book emerges that genuinely deserves our attention, and this is one of those rare finds. It's a resource for everyone—from individuals seeking personal insight to parents, managers, HR professionals, and negotiators. With clear, science-backed guidance from an author with the expertise to make these concepts immediately practical, this book sheds light on the workings of the human mind. It offers tools for enhancing relationships and communication, making it invaluable in both personal and professional spheres.

The Upper Hand offers a fresh and ethical approach to influence, grounded in solid research and proven best practices. Dr. Maroño, an award-winning academic and gifted communicator, artfully combines storytelling with empirical science to share insights that resonate deeply. This isn't about outdated tactics or instilling unnecessary fear, apprehension, or artificial scarcity; rather, it's a guide to harnessing evidence-based, ethical strategies that build trust and foster genuine relationships. Dr. Maroño's expertise shines through

FOREWORD

in every chapter, making complex concepts accessible, practical, and highly relevant for readers across personal and professional realms. From how we speak to the words we choose, you will quickly see that even the smallest of things matter. Your eyes will see the world differently, one in which influence is all around us: subtle, nuanced, pervasive, and inevitably shaping many of our decisions. Knowing these techniques is as important or perhaps even more so than utilizing these techniques.

You don't need a background in science or psychology to grasp the insights offered here, which are refreshingly clear, practical, and easy to apply. With Dr. Maroño's guidance, you'll find yourself building more meaningful connections but also having a greater understanding of the world around you.

While many books offer surface-level insights, *The Upper Hand* stands apart by delving into the biological and neurological foundations of influence, providing a rich, evidence-based perspective that builds confidence in each technique. Dr. Maroño unpacks the science behind social engineering, a term often misunderstood, revealing that it's really about creating meaningful relationships, building lasting foundations, and crafting solutions to social challenges.

This book doesn't just inform; it transforms your understanding of human connection, showing you why these methods work and how to apply them effectively. It may be the most impactful read of the decade, making now the perfect time to explore its insights and practical wisdom.

Whether you're a seasoned professional or just beginning, these principles will elevate your approach to connecting with others. This book is a learning journey, and one that will leave you not only satisfied but genuinely equipped with proven skills for fostering

FOREWORD

cooperation, building trust, and making an impact. Dive into this journey with Dr. Maroño and come away with tools to truly transform your interactions for a lifetime.

—Joe Navarro
Body Language Expert, Bestselling Author

INTRODUCTION

As humans, we have the innate ability to influence others. We are constantly influencing one another, even when we don't know it. How we speak to others, how we dress, and how we interact with the world around us influences how others see us. We even influence people by *not* interacting with them (ever given someone the cold shoulder?).

Influence is the process of affecting others' behaviors, thoughts, or decisions. Most people immediately think of influence as manipulation. But, as a behavioral scientist, I've come to understand there is a distinct difference between the two. And, surprisingly, the most effective influence strategies in today's connected world actually avoid manipulation, coercion, or high-pressure tactics. Instead, they rely on building trust and a desire to cooperate—innate human drives we've shared as a species for millennia.

From my years of neurological, biological, psychological, and forensic research, plus my experience as a practitioner and the trusted insights of my colleagues, I've come to create a framework for connection and influence: The Upper Hand. I've been testing out these practices and principles for years, even before I had names for them. They helped me grow from a struggling PhD student who constantly heard from friends, family, and mentors that my goals were "too ambitious" to achieving a lifelong dream: training agents of the US Secret Service.

The Upper Hand is a framework for using influence through ethical, mutually beneficial means. It takes the current science of human behavior into account, guiding its users through the most effective strategies for influence. Everyone who reads this book will leave with new strategies for connecting with others and making a lasting impact in their lives.

In 2023, a (now retired) supervisory Secret Service agent sent me and my boss, Chris Hadnagy, an email thanking us for helping him gain a full confession from a suspect accused of sexually abusing a minor. It was a shock to both of us. He told us he listened to our podcast, *The Social Engineer*, which aims to help listeners learn more about psychology from various experts in the field. My series, *The Doctor Is In*, consists of Chris and me discussing all things psychology and behavioral science.

On his way in to work, Brad turned on an episode of *The Doctor Is In*—an episode about learned helplessness. In this episode, I mentioned that many individuals who have experienced sexual abuse may attempt to regain a sense of control over their bodies and lives by engaging in hypersexual behavior. It's a maladaptive coping mechanism to reclaim agency over their own sexuality and body.

When Brad heard this, he felt a stroke of inspiration and approached his next interview from a new perspective. That morning, Brad received a full confession from the predator. Then he sent the email to Chris and me, informing us that, thanks to our episode,

INTRODUCTION

a predator would be put away for life. When I responded to Brad's email, I told him I'd be happy to connect with him and offer any additional insights into his work. I was honored to contribute to putting away dangerous predators.

This exchange marked the beginning of an influential relationship between Brad and me. We maintained a strong working relationship. Any time he reached out to me, I was always keen to help. I greatly admired the work he did, and I felt honored to contribute whenever I could.

I didn't help Brad because I wanted anything from him; I helped him because I believed in his work. I believed my expertise could help him build trust with those he interviewed. It may seem hard to believe someone facing a life sentence could come to trust the person interrogating them, but my hope is that, as you read on, you'll come to understand how crucial trust is for any influence strategy. You'll learn about people like former FBI agent and spy catcher Joe Navarro, my good friend and mentor, who still receives messages from people he put in prison—ones who have served their time and now want his advice. He was never unfair or manipulative with the people he interrogated, and they still trust him years later.

Influence, at its core, is about trust. When we ask our friends for advice, we are influenced by their answer because we trust their judgment. When we ask our bosses for help at work, we do so because we trust them to guide us. Our parents influence our morals, beliefs, personalities, and worldview, all because they are the first people in our lives to gain our trust or, sadly for some, lose it. Trust strengthens a person's ability to influence, as well as their chance of success.

Without trust, influence becomes manipulation. Manipulative people affect others through fear, anger, and control. Manipulation is influence without a relationship, without connection, and is therefore an antisocial tactic. Manipulation is only successful when it comes at the cost of other people's well-being. Using manipulation, control, or coercion may work in the short term, but in the end, manipulators are more likely to land on the other end of Brad's interrogation room.

You can form lasting, beneficial relationships without taking advantage of others. Humans are neurologically wired to connect and collaborate, and this innate drive doesn't make us weak or naive. Instead, it positions us to make the most of our relationships.

Influence works best when it builds from an understanding of human biology, psychology, and sociology—a biopsychosocial approach. Rising from amateur status to master influencer means taking a holistic account of what happens to a human inside and outside of their body when they interact with others. To truly gain The Upper Hand, we need every component functioning well, ensuring the comfort, confidence, and competence of every person we influence.

Our interactions with other people influence the trajectory of our lives. Positive interactions lead to genuine connections, grown from a mutual desire to learn, share, and collaborate. These connections can create lasting friendships. They can foster lucrative business relationships. They can even help propel us forward in life in new, unexpected ways. In my own journey, influence helped me establish genuine, meaningful connections with others, who all helped me get where I am today.

After I spent a few months trading knowledge with Brad, he presented Chris and me with a unique opportunity. He told us he was part of a team putting together a training seminar for the Internet Crimes Against Children Task Force Program (ICAC). He wanted us to speak at this training. Chris and I didn't need to think about

INTRODUCTION

it—we jumped at the opportunity right away. Once he knew we were interested, Brad presented our credentials to his supervisor and the ICAC event organizer, who swiftly accepted the proposal. You can imagine our excitement when we received the invitation.

Before we knew it, Chris, Brad, and I were standing center stage, looking out over a sea of special agents: local police, detectives, Secret Service, and Department of Homeland Security agents were all in attendance. I'd love to get specific and tell you some names, but then I'd have to kill you, and then someone would probably have to kill me (kidding, of course).

This training was a dream come true for me, but more than that, it reminded me of the power of influence. These officials gained new strategies for eliciting information by connecting, collaborating, and earning trust. These strategies could save the lives of hundreds, maybe even thousands of children. It could stop the cycle of abuse from carrying on to more generations. The ripple effect of prosocial influence could stretch far beyond that ICAC stage, reaching people I'd never meet, never know, never hear from—but their lives would be fundamentally changed, maybe even saved.

And what I taught in that training only covered a fraction of what you're about to learn.

By the time you reach the end of this book, you'll have new influence strategies to help you master your interactions on a daily basis. You'll learn small-scale influence, the kind that will help you leverage your restaurant choice for lunch with friends. Next time you buy a car, you'll walk off the lot with a better deal than most people have ever heard of. You'll know how to swiftly convince your family to let you host holidays so you don't have to travel (or, if you're not the hosting type, you'll convince someone else to host). You'll come up with hundreds of new strategies for getting what you want from others, all without ever feeling like you're being dishonest or inauthentic.

These small-scale benefits are only the beginning. When used for larger goals, influence can ripple out to touch the lives of countless people. In Brad's case, when he used influence to secure a confession from a predator, he saved children's lives. By preventing the abuse of children, he also made it less likely those children would grow up to continue a cycle of abuse that could have carried on for generations. Influence on a large scale doesn't only make your life better—it makes the world better.

Influence skills, when harnessed with an understanding of the human brain, can also create lifelong benefits. Your reputation as a confident, competent professional who makes others comfortable just by talking with them will ripple out beyond your current reach. Before long, you might end up with new opportunities you didn't even set out for on your own. Whether you're looking to sell more homes as a real estate agent, earn new clients as a consultant, or secure a confession as an investigator, you'll find more success after mastering The Upper Hand. You'll see the patterns of human behavior in every interaction and learn to gracefully steer encounters toward positive outcomes.

After we finished our presentation at the ICAC, audience members approached us with kind words. "This is the best training I have ever been to," one person said. "I already have a plan to put what I've learned here to use," another said. "I've been in law enforcement for 34 years, but I truly believe one can always learn new things, and I learned a lot today. I will put into practice what I learned and pass it on to others." Before we left for the evening, the event facilitators invited us to present again. This time, they asked us to present at their next training in Seattle for a nationwide training event.

INTRODUCTION

We said yes.

I'm still in the early stages of my professional life, yet I know the success I've achieved so far is not from my work alone. Opportunities like the ICAC training come from the relationships I've built with others. The people with whom I've connected, the collaborations we take on together, are the cornerstone of my success. I've climbed to professional heights I never thought I'd see, much less see in my first decade as an expert.

That's the beauty of The Upper Hand at work: my invaluable relationships, in both my professional and personal life, began with a little bit of influence. I've never tricked anyone into thinking I'm someone I'm not. I've never made anyone think I can offer something more than what I have. I've simply strategized ways to put my best foot forward during interactions, ensuring the best parts of myself are available to those who need those skills most. In return, they often do the same for me, not because they feel they have to, but because they want to.

How we interact with other people matters. As we move through this life, we constantly encounter opportunities for influence. The classes we attend, the jobs we take, and the events we attend give us countless chances to change our lives by making new connections with the people we encounter along the way. Despite the innate power of influence, few of us actually spend much time thinking about the best ways to use it. The Upper Hand changes this by helping us understand everyday influence and how to harness it.

In the coming chapters of this book, I will guide you through how to wield The Upper Hand with skill and integrity. You'll learn how to get what you want from others while building and maintaining trust. We'll see how the techniques of The Upper Hand can be applied in all types of situations, from high-stakes boardroom meetings to getting directions from strangers.

You'll learn how to jump-start trust and "Create a Tribe," sometimes with a single comment. You'll learn how the "Speak Their Language" technique can deepen connections and demonstrate your expertise. In the "Pants Yourself" chapter, we'll explore the power of transparency and vulnerability in encouraging cooperation. For the technique "Hold, Don't Squeeze," we'll dissect the stress response that often has us pushing for a close too hard too soon. And in "Shelve It," we'll see how resisting retaliation consistently gives you The Upper Hand.

Influence is powerful, and The Upper Hand is a tool for wielding that power responsibly. As you move through this book, learning the principles and practices within, you'll see how influence can get you what you want without you even needing to ask. That doesn't mean you're playing mind games, nor does it mean you're taking advantage of some hidden flaw in humanity. Instead, it means making the most of your relationships with others. The Upper Hand is about becoming such a positive influence on people, they'll want to collaborate with you however they can, because being a part of something with you is more meaningful than going it alone.

Part I

UNDERSTANDING INFLUENCE

Chapter 1

WIELDING THE UPPER HAND

What does it mean to gain the upper hand on another person? The common responses to this question often center around leveraging something—connections, intelligence, charm, beauty, money, status, or insider knowledge—that gives you an advantage during an interaction. But what do you do if you have none of those things? How do you get what you want? And is it possible to get it without jeopardizing existing and potential relationships?

It is possible to gain the upper hand over someone, even a complete stranger, with no leverage at all. And this is important to note, because leverage isn't failproof. Even if you have an IQ of 180, a face that rivals Helen of Troy, and a loaded Swiss bank account, these traits don't guarantee you'll get what you want from others.

Leverage, by definition, requires some amount of force. Force creates friction in an interaction and erodes trust. There's no guarantee someone will be swayed by the leverage you possess. A developer might offer $50,000 over asking on a property, yet the homeowner sells to a young couple with dreams of raising their children in the home. A former underwear model may lose a client-facing receptionist gig to a dowdy fiftysomething with a little more experience. A parent threatens punishment, but the teenager still disobeys.

When leverage fails, people often turn to tricks and schemes, applying more force rather than laying off the pressure. They might use resource scarcity or time pressure, or take advantage of a power dynamic to drive desired behavior. These tactics can work in the short term, but when they're used over longer periods, such as in modern business dealings, they often ruin relationships. And some of the most important deals require months or even years of cooperation from both parties—which is impossible when one side makes the other feel betrayed.

There is a path you can walk to gain your desired outcome without using manipulative tactics. I call it The Upper Hand.

The Upper Hand is my framework for using influence without resorting to unethical, manipulative persuasion strategies. This framework draws from modern behaviorism to present the most effective strategies for influence. When you use The Upper Hand, you gain the ability to enter a conversation without any leverage at all and still walk away with exactly what you wanted. This framework isn't dishonest, coercive, or even sneaky—in fact, it's more intuitive than any manipulative strategies, because it's built on our natural instinct to trust others.

Mitchell Presnick is a man who intuited how to wield The Upper Hand early in his career. Today, Mitch is an entrepreneur with over 30 years of investing experience in China. He's brought multiple American brands to the massive markets in China, including

Anheuser-Busch, Edelman, Proctor & Gamble, Mars Inc., Johnson & Johnson, and more.

These days, Mitch has a reputation of success he can leverage in his business deals. But back in late 2003, Mitch only had a business plan—one he needed funding and partners for. His idea was to bring a model of business to China it had never practiced before: franchising.

Former colleagues and friends called him crazy—the model was prime for American and Western capitalism, but it would never work in the Chinese economy. Yet Mitch knew there was an opportunity in China, and that the first type of franchise business that would thrive there would be budget hotels. It wasn't sexy, it didn't have the allure franchising, say, the Four Seasons would, but Mitch had a hunch it would work.

Before China hosted budget chain hotels—much less American-brand hotels—all consumers had to go on when assessing a hotel in China was the price. These were the days before websites like Booking.com or Kayak informed guests of what to expect at an independent hotel. A cheap hotel could be immaculate, and an expensive hotel could host more rats than humans. Mitch believed customers wanted consistency more than luxury, that most customers would opt for the comfort and trust of a recognizable brand, even if it cost a little bit more than the average independent Chinese hotel at the time.

To make his dream a reality, Mitch couldn't rely on a flashy slide deck, high-pressure sales tactics, or "creative" numbers. And acting aloof or as if his plan had several bidders lined up would be deceptive. If he was going to secure a partnership, he needed the business leaders to trust him.

He managed to cinch a meeting with representatives from Super

8, but the interaction would be an uphill battle. First, Super 8 had stated they weren't very interested in expanding internationally. Second, the idea of bringing franchising to China wasn't necessarily novel—and it wasn't something he could patent and hold back for another offer. Once Mitch presented the business plan, Super 8 could easily take his idea and enact it on their own, without him. And after sinking two months of time and effort—plus hefty expenses—into research to formulate the business plan, he *really* wanted to be the one to enact it.

Super 8 could swindle the business plan, but Mitch had an ace up his sleeve too: he instinctively knew how to wield The Upper Hand. While Mitch didn't know The Upper Hand by name, he did know enough about people—what they want, how they behave, and how to earn their trust—to wield it during this interaction.

Entering the boardroom, Mitch's hands felt clammy. He set down his materials on the conference table, slyly wiping his hands on his suit before shaking each Super 8 representative's hand. He made sure to ask for each individual's name, even the minutes taker. Immediately after shaking hands, he quickly Created a Tribe (which we'll cover in more detail soon) with the whole room, making a quip about how there were no wet noodles in the room—everyone had strong handshakes, which, he suggested, was a good omen.

Mitch felt a bit lighter seeing smiles and smirks around the room at his comment, and he transitioned into presenting his slide deck. He showcased his expertise by presenting his work with other similar mid-tier brands, using the technique of Speaking Their (Super 8's) Language. He didn't suggest Super 8 would become the next Hilton or Four Seasons—they would remain a dependable, budget-friendly option for consumers in the States—and that's exactly the brand image they would retain abroad. In fact, Mitch pointed out, it was an advantage to be a budget chain to break into the hotel market in China, since many of the country's independent motels had low price points.

The Super 8 team members shifted in their seats. Mitch wasn't sure if it was out of interest or boredom, but they were all looking at his slides. Occasionally a rep would glance at the printed version of his pitch deck in front of them. The only other noise in the room was the scribbling of a pen—the notetaker keeping the minutes.

Mitch forged ahead, addressing the elephant in the room: his lack of direct experience in hotels. This was what he figured would be Super 8's biggest concern when it came to partnering with him. He metaphorically Pantsed Himself by admitting the obvious drawback to him leading the project. However, he told the room, he knew the Chinese market better than anyone else they could hire, and his business plan proved he was more than capable of learning the ropes. He spoke about how he preferred honesty and reliability in his business relationships, and admitting his lack of direct experience was part of that mindset.

When he reached the final slide in his presentation, everyone was leaning forward. Then the screen went black, and the notetaker hopped up to flick the lights on. The body language around the room seemed to indicate a positive response to Mitch's proposal, but it was too soon to make the ask. He knew to squeeze too hard, and ask for a "yes" immediately, would backfire. He used Hold, Don't Squeeze, and backed off, instead trying a completely different route from what most people would use.

"Guys, listen," Mitch said, "I'm either going to leave here today with a signed letter of intent, or I'm going to leave this plan here as a gift to you."

The Super 8 reps exchanged surprised expressions. One opened his mouth to speak, then closed it, frowning. No one quite knew how to respond—it's not every day an entrepreneur makes a pitch, defends its probability of success, and then offers to give it away for free. Was this some sort of trick?

Mitch saw the unspoken question hanging in the air. It was time to squeeze, just a little.

"Don't get me wrong—I want to lead this project," he clarified. "I know I'm the one who can make it happen. But I want to see this brand in China whether I introduce it or not. Franchising is part of China's future. Economy hotel chains are part of China's future. This plan proves it."

The Super 8 team shared another round of glances before one representative spoke.

"Mitch, I have a feeling you'll leave with a signed letter of intent," he said, tearing a piece of legal paper off its pad. He clicked his pen. "Let's discuss what that letter says. Take a seat."

By the time the meeting ended, Mitch had a signed letter of intent. Within a year, he secured the rights to build up Super 8 hotels in China. Within five years, under Mitch's supervision, Super 8 grew into one of the largest economy chains in the country.[1] It was a long-term, mutually beneficial outcome for both parties.

When I interviewed Mitch about his story, I noticed his attitude toward Super 8 differed from how many people think about influencing others. Many people assume getting what they want is a zero-sum game, and so to influence is to engage in a battle that will result in winners and losers. Yet Mitch's viewpoint was and is different.

"This isn't misdirection. It's not deception. It's curation," Mitch told me. "I didn't go into the deal trying to prove who was right and who was wrong . . . we're both right by the end."

Mitch wasn't trying to "beat" the Super 8 boardroom—he wanted them to cooperate.

Back in 2003, Mitch didn't have much leverage, but he knew how to build trust, connect with others, inspire confidence, and gauge his own pressure. Wielding The Upper Hand isn't magic—it taps into the same principles of influence and persuasion humans have used for millennia. The difference is the techniques of The Upper Hand make the framework act more like a hand of guidance than a hand of force.

Business deals often feel like mind games, but we don't have to resort to cutthroat strategies or dishonest tactics to seal a deal, raise capital, or win contracts. Understanding the science behind effective influence can help anyone gain The Upper Hand in any interaction, whether that's closing a deal, convincing grandma to give up driving, or having an excellent first date.

Gaining The Upper Hand in any interaction is not about exploitation or leveraging force but rather establishing trust and engaging the human instinct to cooperate. Understanding the foundational principles of human behavior will empower you to navigate both personal and professional situations effectively, creating interactions where everyone wins.

Deconstructing the Myth of Influence

There is a motto where I work: "Leave others feeling better for having met you."

As the Director of Education at Social-Engineer LLC, I follow the company's motto in all my work. Our CEO, Chris Hadnagy, set up this motto to be a guiding light in the world of influence and social engineering. Our engineers reveal system and security weaknesses for clients by using manipulation, coercion, and high-pressure tactics—all methods The Upper Hand avoids. When you spend half your days pretending to live on the dark side of social engineering, it can be tough to find your way back to the light. Chris's motto helps keep everyone at Social-Engineer aligned with an ethical approach to their duties.

When you dive into the world of social engineering and influence, there are temptations everywhere. Securing the "yes" through ethical, meaningful, and mutually beneficial means can feel tedious. If you're not laser-focused on maintaining morality, it's all too easy to slide into manipulation. When the time comes to choose between prosocial influence or coercion, I find myself repeating: "leave others feeling better for having met you."

So what is influence exactly, and how does it differ from social engineering? While many of us have undoubtedly heard the word "influence" in dozens of contexts, our idea of what it means in a biopsychosocial context may be a bit skewed. The word "influence" has taken on a negative connotation over the last few decades. Social media's propagation of "influencers" makes us think of vapid, low-effort salespeople pushing products in obvious and sometimes subliminal posts. Being "under the influence" of a substance or person conjures the idea of not being in control of our own actions.

It's difficult to say influence in and of itself is positive or negative. Humans influence one another every day. How you answer the phone influences how the caller responds. When you give advice to a trusted friend, you may influence their decisions. When you make silly faces at a wailing baby, you attempt to influence their mood in hopes that the baby smiles, laughs, or at least stops crying. These instances of influence aren't malicious or selfish—they pepper our daily lives with meaning and connection.

Since influence itself is neither wholly positive nor negative, most people will say the *way* we influence others is either positive or negative. Influencing and being influenced is inescapable, but there is a line between ethical and unethical methods of influence. Putting someone in a state of stress where that pressure can induce a "yes" is unethical. But being transparent, presenting options, and then receiving a "yes" is perfectly ethical.

When we think about what it means to influence others, many of us shy away from the idea. We think influencing someone else means breaching their trust. However, influence is only successful because others trust us.

Social engineering is an oft-misunderstood subcategory of influence. Chris has a clear definition for the term, and he's been using it for the last few decades: "Social engineering is any act that influences a person to take an action that may or may not be in their best interest."[2] The definition is broad because social engineering isn't always positive or negative. Sometimes, social engineering helps "human hackers" break into secure systems, from email addresses to government networks. Other times, social engineering helps crisis counselors calm down a victim to help them start their healing process.

Social engineering is a practice for eliciting information from others—and with the power to draw out information (of all kinds) comes great responsibility. Information elicitation on its own is not inherently good or evil. Manipulating a situation to extract a social security number from a victim to use in fraudulent activities is obviously unethical. However, eliciting information from a stranger in a waiting room about where they're from, why they're waiting, and what kind of movies they like is simply the beginning of a connection.

Many people only consider social engineering's negative tactics. And it's true that con artists and fraudsters do sometimes employ principles of social engineering. Creating a situation rife with panic, fear, and confusion *is* social engineering. However, the crucial separation between positive and negative social engineering is the *intention* behind the act. If someone uses social engineering to swindle another person, their intention is unethical, but that doesn't make the method morally wrong. Without factoring intention, social engineering may sound like subterfuge, but it really depends on the goal.

Say, for example, you want to buy a friend the perfect surprise birthday gift. Using techniques from social engineering, it's possible to find out what they want without asking outright. You can find indirect, unsuspecting ways to ask what they might want (or need). When you're over at their house next, you might notice they use a beat-up cheese grater, possess a rusty watering can, and are self-conscious about their lack of throw pillows and blankets. The next time the two of you are talking decor, you ask guiding questions that reveal their aesthetic preferences and how frequently they shred cheese. You might note that they're highly accident-prone, so a cheese grater with an added safety mechanism is the best choice. After some first-class noticing and social engineering to elicit information, you can be confident in which gift will produce the most delight. This is social engineering used for good—otherwise known as prosocial engineering.

Prosocial engineering involves purposely influencing another person toward cooperation without the intention to cause psychological harm. In the personal and professional realm, opportunities for influence appear on a daily basis. Influencing your boss to let you take on more responsibility could lead to a resume and salary boost for you, and your boss being able to go home by six o'clock instead of eight. Mending a rift between two colleagues could mean less drama in your day-to-day work life. Persuading a friend who loves ramen to try pho could open up their palate to a whole new cuisine—and if they hate it, now you know for sure you'll need to find another friend if you want to try the next new pho restaurant that opens. Knowing the benefits you reap from interactions go hand in hand with others' rewards—this is how you become a prosocial engineer. The choices we make define who we are, who we will be, and how others see us.

Prosocial engineers recognize the value in understanding fundamental human desires for connection, safety, and valuable relationships. They approach all interactions from an empathetic, cooperative perspective. They want more than a transaction with the people they influence—they want a long-lasting collaboration that reaps rewards for both sides. Prosocial engineers don't convince others to work *for* them; they convince others to work *with* them to reach a shared goal.

A prosocial engineer operates like a gardener in their greenhouse, fostering each relationship based on what best helps it grow. Each plant in the greenhouse has different needs—soil density, water tolerance, sunlight sensitivity—but the basic principles of plant growth are the same. Similarly, even though every human has a unique perspective, experience, and drive, the fundamental functions of our brains are the same. Botany helps us understand how plants thrive and grow. Psychology helps us understand how other humans think. That's why The Upper Hand works—it's the hand that encourages growth in the form of thriving, cooperative relationships.

Instead of aiming to control interactions, prosocial engineers aim to shape the flow of conversation toward mutual success. No one can fully control every factor of an interaction without coercive control—it would be as impossible as growing a tree without light, water, or soil. Instead, prosocial engineers arm themselves with knowledge about how to best encourage growth, then adapt their strategies to make sure their efforts are fruitful.

Prosocial engineers leave others better off, just for the simple act of meeting them.

At Social-Engineer, we keep this mantra front and center because of the nature of our work. Many of our engineers teach clients about social engineering by showing them how it can be used against them. The analysts hack into systems, elicit personal information, and emulate real-world attacks, all to help clients find their vulnerabilities. It's tempting to resort to unethical practices for the sake of training—after all, that's what the real bad guys would do—but we avoid making clients feel vulnerable or discriminated against, since doing so would make them too uncomfortable to learn from us. By keeping the company motto in mind, we all remember to focus on education, not manipulation.

Over the years, as I've moved through the world of social engineering, I recognized how little the average person knows about their own susceptibility. Most people lack a fundamental understanding of how social engineering tactics can subtly influence them into giving up sensitive information. Although most people know not to share their date of birth, social security number, or bank account information with strangers, if they're convinced of someone's trustworthiness (or benign-ness), that knowledge fails to protect them.

I decided to write a book on influence and social engineers because I want people to know themselves and others better—what makes us open to sharing, willing to cooperate, and apprehensive about working with others. I want them to see signs of manipulation before it's too late. And when it comes to practicing influence techniques in their own lives, I want people to feel like they can be effective without being unethical. That's why I developed The Upper Hand.

The Upper Hand framework enables prosocial engineers to transition from principle understanding to tactical application, drawing a firm line between ethical influence and manipulation. The framework provides the tools you need to succeed without crossing that line. Gaining The Upper Hand in any interaction is not about exploitation or leveraging force, but rather establishing trust and engaging the human instinct to cooperate. Understanding the foundational principles of human behavior will empower you to navigate both personal and professional situations effectively, creating interactions where everyone wins.

Mastering prosocial influence takes practice. At Social-Engineer, every new employee—whether they're intending to become a social engineer or working in IT—attends an intensive week of training sessions. This helps all of us better understand influence, social engineering, and information elicitation, preparing us to protect ourselves from malicious influence and ethically influence others.

During each training session, we were given homework assignments to help us practice prosocial engineering in and out of the workplace. These assignments grew tougher as the sessions went on. One early assignment asked us to find a stranger, strike up a conversation, and learn their last name, birthday, and reason for visiting Orlando by the end of our interaction. Another asked us to learn a secret from a stranger. A final (and tricky) assignment asked us to get an answer to the question: "What's your biggest regret in life?" Every assignment required us to gain the trust of a stranger and connect with them on a level deeper than most first interactions go.

I'm not a social engineer by trade, but I know the principles of influence well enough to incorporate them into my everyday life. Small-scale influence builds larger influence. Like with any skill, the more you practice, the better you perform. It's difficult to imagine finding out a stranger's biggest regret now, but after some practice, you'll be surprised how easily people willingly share intimate information with you. When you present yourself as a kind, trustworthy, cooperative person, people won't just accept your influence—they'll actively seek out your input.

"Leaving people better for having met you" can sound like a tall order because it requires being in touch with the intention preceding the influence. Sometimes intentions are obvious and easy to evaluate. To Super 8, Mitch's intentions were clear: sure, he was motivated by his own professional success, but his presentation didn't focus on only his success. He focused instead on his genuine desire to bring reliable accommodation to the millions and billions of citizens and tourists in China. There's nothing wrong with admitting how you stand to benefit in an interaction—in fact, avoiding selfish intentions will only damage trust. The key is to acknowledge what you stand to gain, then ensure your focus remains on mutual benefits stemming from ethical intentions. When ethical intentions are clear, trust comes easier. And this is crucial, because—as you'll read in the next nine chapters—trust is the foundation of influence.

Trust: The Foundation of Influence

Wielding The Upper Hand requires a solid understanding of trust's role in any interaction. Though the human brain is wired to cooperate and connect with others, it's also wired to avoid the untrustworthy. If the brain senses false trust or manipulation, attempts at influence can dramatically backfire.

In the US TV show *The Office*,[3] Andy Bernard is the perfect example of influence backfiring. When he first appears, Andy brags to the camera about his ability to influence his new coworkers by using basic manipulation tactics: "name repetition, personality mirroring, and never breaking off a handshake." He sees some initial success from these tactics, but it doesn't take long for his officemates to see through his ploy. Once they recognize his influence as fake, they dislike him, and it takes a long time for him to earn their trust again.

In the real world, it takes more than a few gimmicks to convince people to trust you, listen to you, and ultimately cooperate with you long term. Leverage such as a power dynamic can be intimidating enough to force temporary cooperation, but it creates a fragile relationship. As soon as the dynamic shifts, the relationship may end, and the barriers to forming a new, equal relationship are higher.

Popular media often portrays influence as a means to strong-arm others into agreement. When Andy's initial influence attempts don't win over his coworker Dwight Schrute, he tries to convince Dwight that he is actually Dwight's superior. (Spoiler alert if you haven't seen *The Office*: it doesn't work. Also, who hasn't seen *The Office* by now?) Myths surrounding influence often relate it to social shortcuts, tricks, and manipulative tactics, condemning it to fail and cause long-term adverse effects on relationships and self-worth.

When I first started my undergraduate program in psychology, I believed influence was mostly a negative concept too. I was convinced people were primed for deception. I believed people were innately selfish. One person would happily disadvantage another for better chances of survival, and so everyone always had to be on the lookout for liars and cheats. But as I began my doctoral degree at the

United Kingdom's University of Lancaster, the research in the field of social psychology suggested otherwise.

Yes, the human brain is wired to survive at all costs. However, our survival is better guaranteed in a group setting, where we can pool resources and benefit from one another's skills. Every human needs connection with and cooperation from other humans to survive and thrive.

In fact, humans are some of the most cooperative animals on the planet. Other animals do cooperate with each other, but many other social mammals typically keep their cooperation limited to relatives or packmates. Humans cooperate with total strangers every day: we pile into buses and planes together, wait in lines at the pharmacy together, and drive cars according to the shared rules of the road. We might not always benefit from cooperating with others (it might cost us an extra minute in the queue), but we do it anyway.

Why?

The short answer is that humans are an extremely social species. Our brains are wired to identify with social groups, like families, communities, and societies. Our chances of survival are greater when we're in a group—there is safety in the herd. The more positive connections an individual has, the more resources are at their disposal, so the greater their chance of survival.

The human brain (and body) contains a complex reward system that floods us with feel-good hormones like oxytocin when we cooperate. When we spend too much time alone, we suffer on a neurochemical level, with increased levels of cortisol, a major stress hormone, in our bloodstream. Fortunately, cortisol, or stress, can be mitigated by oxytocin, typically labeled as the "love hormone" but more aptly recognized as the "social trust" hormone.[4] We'll be exploring this in more depth in the next chapter.

Oxytocin plays a role in every person-to-person interaction. When two people, even strangers, cooperate with each other, they each get a boost of oxytocin. The brain feels safe and rewards us with a specific sensation. Even watching two people cooperate can give us an oxytocin boost. The phrase "faith in humanity restored" is often repeated after watching one person do a good deed for another—and the feeling that stimulates that turn of phrase is likely a little oxytocin boost.

Thousands of studies have centered around why humans are so keen to cooperate, but in 2023, a group of scientists wanted a more holistic view.[5] They had questions about the consistency of cooperation, like: What qualities make a person more cooperative? Are some people cooperative in certain situations but uncooperative in others? Similarly, are some people more likely to inspire cooperation in others? Are there people who are naturally *un*cooperative? To better understand the nature of cooperation, these scientists designed an experiment to test its limits.

The scientists went into the experiment knowing how vital trust is in any human interaction. Additional research has shown that when people decide to cooperate with each other, they consciously and unconsciously suss out the other person. The human brain makes split-second judgments on prosocial traits like trustworthiness, generosity, and competence. It takes our brains about 33 milliseconds to decide whether another person appears trustworthy.[6] Once our brains determine an individual is trustworthy, we're more likely to cooperate with them.

The experimenters determined the best way to test effects on cooperation was to put subjects through a series of games. They designed 10 different games for the subjects to play. Each game covertly tested how personalization affects prosocial behavior. That is, how the degree of familiarity between two players affected their willingness to cooperate. The experimenters wanted to find out if knowing the other players in the game would lead a subject to cooperate at higher rates. Just as it's harder to leave spiteful comments on a close friend's social media post, it's often more difficult to treat an opponent badly if you see their face and know who they are.

Since each study participant was subject to the same rules, let's look at the game experiments through the eyes of a single participant: we'll call her Donna. Before she started to play, Donna had her photo taken. Then, she was asked a few questions in front of a camera. The video would not have sound, they told her—it was simply for identification purposes.

Then, Donna sat down in front of a computer and saw a set of six other players' photos. She scored the photos on a scale of 1–5 (1 being the lowest) for eight traits: generous, trustworthy, rational, risk-taking, greedy, angry, happy, and attractive.

Once the person-scoring was finished, the games began. The first game was called The Dictator Game, and the prompt appeared on Donna's computer (paraphrased for simplicity):

> *You have 100 points (money) in your pocket when you meet a person in need on the street. They tell you they need money to get back on their feet, and their request equates to exactly 100 points. Now you have to decide how much to give this person, if anything at all. Please notice that your interaction partner (the person in need) is a real participant in this experiment. All the points you give them will be transferred to them, and all the points you keep will stay with you.*

For the first round, Donna had to choose how many points to give each player. For the second round, before she made her decision,

WIELDING THE UPPER HAND

Donna watched a 20-second video of the person in need before making a choice. The video was a silent clip of Donna's partner chatting with one of the scientists. Donna noticed her partner's kind eyes and soft smile. The third round presented her with a video of a new stranger—a new partner—with rosy cheeks and a big, goofy grin.

The rest of the games followed the same pattern: Donna read the rules and chose an outcome. Each game was modeled after a real-life scenario; Donna played as a peach vendor, a lottery winner, and a long-distance cyclist. The first round of each game gave no information about her partner, and the next two rounds gave her video clips of the person on the other end of the game.

Donna's results—along with the results for the other 180 participants—revealed that seeing the video clips of other players influenced her cooperation. Donna distributed points more generously after seeing videos, as did the other players in the game. When her partners saw her face during the games, they were more cooperative and generous, knowing she was on the other end. (The results also suggest this group of strangers was adept at accurately guessing a person's level of generosity from just a photo.)

None of the participants had to give away their points, but many did, particularly after seeing videos of the other players. Just a small bit of connection—a video of a person—induced a bump in generosity toward others. In essence, it was easier for participants to say "yes" to giving away their points when they felt higher levels of trust. (It's important to note that other studies have shown the opposite can be true too: when trust is broken, retaliation occurs—more on this in the coming chapters.)

Not everyone will trust you or cooperate with you all the time. If it were that easy, we could point-blank ask for what we want and consistently receive it. Part of what makes influence tricky—especially in business—is knowing there will be resistance. There are hoops to jump through to approve budgets. There are processes for how to implement new tools. There are protocols for how to hire new employees. You can't ask for a rule to change and expect it to change for you, because it's a rule that doesn't only affect you.

When you craft a pitch or guide a business interaction, you prepare to meet resistance ahead of time. Yes, people are inclined to cooperate with each other, but it's still a risk-versus-reward situation. In Mitch's case, he knew he had a business plan that would benefit Super 8, yet it was still a risk for the Super 8 team to work with him, someone they had known for only several hours. Mitch needed to quickly build trust and encourage cooperation to chip away at their resistance and secure a "yes." He knew the business game, and he knew how to ensure everyone playing could win.

In any game, from freeze tag to canasta, there is one rule so basic that most instructions don't even include it: *the players must trust each other*. In a game of chess, you must trust your opponent isn't using outside help to strategize. If you're playing go fish, you must trust the other players to be honest about the cards in their hands. And if you're sharing information with someone new, you must trust they won't use it to cheat you. Trust is a central component of all interactions, because it is crucial to overcoming resistance.

A Prosocial Game

Every new interaction is a game. The rules follow a basic risk-versus-reward pattern: you give information—a risk—in hopes of receiving a helpful response—a reward. In a job interview, you provide information about your professional life in hopes of "winning" a job offer. On a first date, you give information about yourself in hopes of "winning" a relationship—or at least a second date. When you tell your doctor about the strange symptoms you're experiencing, you're hoping to "win" a diagnosis and a treatment plan.

When you approach interactions with the sole intent of coming out the winner, you add a new rule: someone has to be the loser. But not all interactions must end with a winner and a loser. In fact, the best interactions are the ones where everyone wins. A successful interview ends with both the interviewer and interviewee feeling excited about their interaction. A great first date means both people enjoyed their time together. A successful medical appointment ends with a satisfied patient and a doctor who has completed a job well done.

The Upper Hand is an influence strategy for "winning" interactions without requiring a "loser." I've spent years studying non-verbal communication, trust, and the psychological mechanisms underpinning human decision-making. I've learned even the most high-stakes, stressful interactions can end in a mutually beneficial agreement. And I designed the techniques of The Upper Hand to promote influence without stealing, scamming, or coercing someone else.

Gaining The Upper Hand requires strict ethical values—it's a form of prosocial engineering. Prosocial engineering is as it sounds—it's the positive side of social engineering. It involves purposely influencing another person toward cooperation without the intention to cause psychological harm. It is devoid of any negative intentions, and works to advance the collective good, not exploit it. In the personal and professional realm, opportunities for influence appear on a daily basis. We are presented with situations we could benefit from, and we must make decisions that either help or hurt us, and help or hurt others. The choices we make define who we are, who we will be, and how others see us.

In a world where companies and customers, business associates, interested parties, and stakeholders are more connected than ever before, it's essential to make use of The Upper Hand. Positive interactions (business reviews, references, etc.) come from prosocial engineering strategies. Sticking to ethical influence techniques leads to better long-term relationships and more beneficial outcomes, which serve our best interest for decades.

And when we secure a "yes," it's not a coerced, tentative "... sure." It's a "Hell yes, let's do it!"

Throughout this book, we'll dive into the latest persuasion science and dissect how the current literature doesn't go far enough to explain how many of the traditional influence tactics actually work (and why in certain situations they fail outright).

But before we can get into all of that, we need to address a common *resistance* to adopting social engineering and influence strategies: the pervasive myth that using any form of influence means manipulating others. The field of influence is sometimes overshadowed by the dark, dirty, and downright devious tactics used by con artists and swindlers. Before we can fully explore the light side of influence—prosocial engineering—we must be aware of what happens on the dark side.

Chapter 2

THE DARK SIDE OF SOCIAL ENGINEERING

Social engineering is a popular weapon for con artists, manipulators, and gaslighters who wish to win over their marks by nefarious means. They use influence tactics to gain a mark's trust, then swindle, emotionally harm, or take advantage of them. Their stories are passed along in hopes that the more people there are who know about their schemes, the fewer people will fall for them.

We can't let swindlers, fraudsters, and manipulators mar the reputation of social engineering and persuasion. Instead, we can combat their negative influence by learning to recognize their go-to techniques. Once we see how *not* to use influence, we're better positioned to see how to use it properly for positive, ethical gains.

Influence and social engineering rely on trust. Gaining trust quickly and easily is a skill that can be used for good or for evil. In the hands of a grade school teacher, championship softball coach, or visionary entrepreneur, this talent can be the difference between making an impact or falling flat. However, in the hands of someone with negative intentions, like a con artist, a white-collar criminal, or a fraudster, misplaced trust can lead to serious harm. Gaining trust through honest means requires similar skills and techniques to gaining trust dishonestly. What differs is how the trust is used once it's gained. By studying people who have made a living off abusing others' trust, we can learn their most common techniques and avoid falling prey to them ... or repeating them.

William Fink, a wealthy real estate man, was on a business trip to Miami in the year 1908.[1] On the train south, he ventured to the bar car and struck up a conversation with a fascinating man named James Ryan. Fink discovered Ryan, like himself, had grown up in Kansas City. They spoke of their shared fondness for French cooking. And, it turned out, they had booked the same hotel in Miami. The more they talked, the more Fink liked Ryan. They had so much in common and seemed to have similar tastes.

After checking in that afternoon, they decided to grab dinner together in the hotel restaurant. The conversation jumped from business to politics to family life. Ryan was extremely well traveled and had been to many of the same places as Fink. The two men joked and laughed together well into the night. And at the end of the meal, Ryan graciously picked up the check.

As they were getting up to leave, Ryan kicked something under the table with his foot. Stooping down, he discovered a billfold lying on the floor.

"Someone forgot their wallet!" he said, eyes wide. "Should we look inside to determine whose it is?" He looked up at Fink, who nodded.

In the wallet, the men found $400 in cash. There was also a

membership card for a prestigious-looking social club, with a full name on it.

"We ought to get this back to its owner, don't you think?" Ryan asked.

"Yes, certainly," Fink responded. "Perhaps we might inquire at the front desk as to whether the wallet's owner is staying here at the hotel."

"That's a fine idea," Ryan beamed.

Fink and Ryan spent nearly eight hours together, and over the course of their partnership, Fink grew convinced of Ryan's trustworthiness. Back in the early 1900s, keeping $400 in a wallet equated to about $12,000 in today's money. Anyone who could turn away a clear opportunity to gain without consequence must be trustworthy.

The trust Fink placed in his new companion was exactly what Ryan needed. While Fink believed he'd met a true friend, Ryan had other plans for their relationship: a popular long con called "the payoff," in which he and several other con men would go on to swindle Fink of $25,000 (over $750,000 in today's dollars).

The trust Ryan earned from Fink seemed genuine, when in reality, it was carefully curated for manipulation. Influence always begins with building trust and confidence in initial interactions. Ryan fooled Fink into believing they had plenty of commonalities: they were on the same train, they were headed to the same hotel, they both loved French cuisine, etc. What Fink didn't know was that he'd been a mark on Ryan's radar for months. Ryan purposely ended up on his train, and he intentionally booked a room at Fink's hotel. He'd done his research on Fink ahead of time, which allowed him to play the part of Fink's perfect match.

After his initial influence strategy went perfectly, Ryan finalized his efforts with a demonstration of trustworthiness. When Ryan suggested they turn the wallet in, he proved he was a man of integrity. This final act solidified his perceived trustworthiness.

Trust is a powerful force when it comes to influence, and sometimes we don't know it's been misplaced until it's too late.

Fink was so convinced of Ryan's trustworthiness that he had no trouble following him to the tracks the next day and placing a bet on a "sure thing" horse. Ryan asked Fink to cover the initial $25,000 bet, promising the payout would be well worth it. When the horse won, Fink felt even more assured in his judgment. It wasn't until Ryan recommended they bet their new winnings on the *next* horse that Fink caught on to his mistake. But by then, the final race results were called, Ryan had disappeared, and the money was gone. Only then did Fink realize his error in judgment.

For the rest of his life, Fink struggled to make business deals with others. Not only did Ryan irreparably damage Fink's trust in him—he damaged Fink's trust in *anyone*. Every person he met made Fink remember his old "friend" and caused him to blush with shame. Rather than risk another letdown, he decided he'd never fully trust anyone again. His past, present, and future relationships suffered as a result.

Over a hundred years later, people are still irreparably damaged every day by all sorts of fraudsters—from mediums and fortune tellers to Ponzi schemers and cult leaders. These people make a show out of their trustworthiness, then rob their victims blind over the course of weeks, months, or years. They use social engineering for their own gain and perpetuate the myth that all influence is dangerous.

The tactics of The Upper Hand do incorporate trust, because trust is necessary to wield any kind of influence. However, what sets this framework apart is its intention: The Upper Hand requires *real*, *earned trust* instead of perceived trust. There's no lying about your trustworthiness when you're prosocially influencing another person.

When influence becomes exploitation, influence becomes unethical. Influence's shady reputation comes from those who exploit trust and confidence through manipulation. They convince people to act outside their own best interest. They influence with intent to cause harm.

The Progression of Control

Trust is the first step in most forms of manipulation, and the easiest way to earn it is through word of mouth. We trust a real estate agent because a friend recommended them. We trust a business coach because another CEO recommended them. We trust the new employee because we trust the hiring officer.

Modern-day fraudsters like Bernie Madoff, a man who defrauded thousands of investors via his wealth management firm, use similar tactics to cult leaders and con artists. Madoff recruited his victims through referrals from wealthy individuals. If your ultra-rich friend introduces you to their trusted financial advisor, you're probably not going to question their authenticity too closely. Madoff also met his marks through exclusive clubs reserved for high-net-worth people. The victims likely assumed, if he's in this club, he must be legit.

The quickest and easiest way to gain someone's trust is to borrow it. When you meet a new person through a mutually trusted acquaintance, like a friend, family member, or colleague, you're much more likely to appear trustworthy. Despite the fact that a mutual connection doesn't equate to trustworthiness, our brains are more comfortable accepting the unfamiliar when it's introduced by the familiar. Criminals and manipulators know this, and they use it to their advantage.

Madoff had a reputation for being selective with his business partners. He chose his marks solely through internal referrals. This made him appear more trustworthy upon first meeting. He would present his marks with an investment opportunity, and he would emphasize they were only receiving the offer because they came highly recommended. He made a show of selecting them, recruiting them, and securing their money to make them feel valuable. His investors were members of an exclusive club, and if you're lucky enough to hear an offer, you'd better jump at the chance to be included, no questions asked.

Since Madoff "earned" trust through existing connections, his victims were more likely to make concessions for his unethical behaviors. When he didn't deliver on his promises, his marks were hesitant to call him out. They carried on without raising an alarm, lest they appear untrustworthy to either the person who referred them to Bernie or to Bernie himself. Meanwhile, he made off with millions by taking control of their trust.

This is how unethical social engineers create long cons: they create a progression of control. Their tactics begin with small signs of perceived trustworthiness—returning a full wallet, relying on friendly references—and take advantage of that trust to convince their marks to act certain ways. The more a mark trusts them, the more they can encourage the mark to act on their behalf. That's how the fraudsters take control, one tiny concession at a time.

Criminals aren't the only manipulators familiar with the progression of control. Entire organizations take advantage of perceived trustworthiness to manipulate people into giving up their time, money, and energy for little to no reward. Toxic corporate environments often follow this pattern, and without interference, those environments can turn downright cultish.

First, the leadership team works to gain a new employee's trust, often aided by internal referral programs. A candidate is referred by a trustworthy connection, and they transfer that trust from their connection to the company itself. Once the candidate is hired, they're more willing to trust the company, since they were introduced through a trusted connection. The company works to maintain that trust at first; they make the candidate feel special, and they offer opportunities for promotions, benefits, and more—as long as the candidate demonstrates loyalty.

When you unknowingly join a corporate cult, you're influenced to fall in line with its culture from day one—it's how you keep your job, which is how you keep putting food on the table. If a company culture doesn't promote individualism, creativity, or expressive freedom, you're quick to pick up a "don't rock the boat" mentality. You fall in line for safety and security. Meanwhile, the company's control grows, and no one inside is brave enough to address it.

Take Sue, for example. When Sue signed on as a data analyst at MegaCo, she couldn't wait for her first day. Her interview was exciting—the CEO even stopped in to greet her in person! All signs pointed to the perfect position, and she trusted this company to value her as an employee. To say she was optimistic would be an understatement.

When she sat down at her desk on that first morning, there was a T-shirt with the company logo folded neatly for her. Underneath was a copy of the employee handbook. The company's mission was plastered across the front: "Big Benefits for the Little Guy." Sue loved that her new job cared so much about the average, everyday person. She thought of herself as a giver, and she felt right at home when she saw MegaCo wanted to give too.

Every person Sue met on her first day was kind and welcoming. They all swore by their jobs, saying MegaCo was the best company in the world.

"I don't even know what I'd do without this job," said the receptionist. "It's the best job I've ever had."

The personal sacrifices started small: Sue tried to be the first one in the office and the last one out. However, her coworkers were doing the same thing, so it wasn't uncommon for Sue to be at her desk from 7 AM to 7 PM. She skipped lunch here and there to deliver a product before its deadline. She memorized the company's slogan and mission statement, which was helpful, because her manager gave her a "company pop quiz" every few weeks.

Before she knew it, Sue found herself a member of a corporate cult. There was no sign of coercion on the surface, only collaboration. It felt great to work in a place where everyone was on the same page, striving toward the same goal. Sue was rewarded for her dedication with kind words, small bonuses, and extra perks like coffee vouchers and coupons for the in-office masseuse.

Her managers dangled an ever-upcoming promotion as long as she kept up the good work. Sue felt like a sucker on the inside, but she was too nervous to say so. She really wanted that promotion. Whenever anyone asked about her job, she said the same thing she heard on her first day: it's the best one she's ever had.

Sue's situation is probably familiar to most people: it's easy to make one concession at a time, not noticing how much is given up incrementally. It's not that people shouldn't make concessions or compromise. However, being aware of these concessions helps us avoid sneaking influence.

When we neglect to notice and accurately label our concessions, we can fall right into the palm of someone's hand. Often, the manipulator will isolate their marks, so the options appear few and far between. Sue invested so much in her job that it became extra difficult to leave. Quitting would mean giving up not just her livelihood, but also her lifestyle, social circle, and a large part of her identity.

This is where misplacing trust in the wrong person, group, or organization can be dangerous. But it's hard to determine where to place trust, especially when it comes to the manipulators who know how to hijack our natural inclination to make connections. When a person escalates to isolating another human being psychologically, this is a very clear indication of the most devious kind of manipulation.

The Psychology of Manipulation

Manipulative people take advantage of the psychological mechanisms that encourage humans to share, cooperate, and connect. They hack the trust system. They tap into our natural prosocial instincts to develop relationships, and take advantage of our natural interest in positive outcomes. It's difficult to convince another person to put themselves at risk for no reason, so manipulators influence how their marks think about the possible rewards.

No person who is well versed in manipulation reveals controlling tendencies at the start of a relationship—that would eliminate trust. Instead, they only present their most charming traits. They appear kind, supportive, and empathetic. They swear that as long as you stay loyal to them, they will stay loyal to you. You trust them because you're psychologically inclined to do so. After all, your friend trusts them. And they are in the same social club as you are.

The first psychological mechanism that manipulators want to suppress is critical thought. Critical thought invites doubt, withholding, and suspicion, which are thought processes that threaten manipulation attempts. Some of the most susceptible targets for manipulation are people without sharp critical thinking skills or with heightened naïveté, because they don't question a kind-presenting person. These victims also typically give the manipulator the benefit of the doubt.

The critical thought process in our brains isn't instant. We respond to new information emotionally before we respond logically. This happens because when we receive new information, it's first processed through the amygdala—the part of the brain that evokes an emotional response. Then, the information is passed to the prefrontal cortex for interpretation. This process is why we sometimes act before we think in high-stress or emotionally charged situations. Taking a step back from an emotional impulse and waiting for the critical thought process helps us make better decisions—but manipulators know this, and they'll do their best to bypass it.

Manipulators try to bypass critical thinking by stopping the thought process *before* the prefrontal cortex responds. They evoke an emotional response in their victims, then follow it with a quick, high-pressure decision. For example, a psychic waves their hands and says, "I see a man with a bald head and a round belly. He wants to speak with you." You picture your late grandfather. But before you realize that this description applies to *most* older men, the psychic follows up with, "He says he loves you and misses you. Do you want to speak with him?"

This suppression strategy is often a go-to tool for cult leaders. They use this tactic to test the loyalty of their followers. They ask for demonstrations of trust, like cutting off contact with the outside world, shaving your head, or committing a crime on their behalf. Before you can think critically about what they're asking, they shut down your thought process by accusing you of disloyalty. That triggers a new emotional response—fear of rejection. The leader threatens your bond, but they make it seem like *you're* the one putting it at risk. By taking advantage of how your brain processes information, the leader manipulates you into acting in ways you wouldn't normally consider.

Another psychological process that can be hijacked is the brain's reward system. Manipulators take advantage of the human brain's neural reward network to "retrain" their victims' perception of the world. The more your brain rewards you during interactions with a manipulator, the more bonded you feel to them, and the less likely you are to break your perceived connection.

Every human brain contains a neural reward network. Specifically, the ventral striatum (VS), the orbitofrontal cortex (OFC), and the amygdala (alongside some smaller regions working in the background) work together to reward us for positive social interactions. The VS anticipates how rewarding the interaction may be and activates accordingly. The amygdala is responsible for measuring the intensity of an interaction as it happens. The OFC determines how positive the interaction is for us. The more positive, intense, and potentially rewarding the interaction, the more we experience a flood of positive hormones.[2]

Since humans are a social species, our brains' reward networks are extremely active when we experience cooperation. Whether we're showing signs of cooperation or perceiving them from an interaction partner, our reward networks light up when they see potential for connection through cooperation. Working toward a shared goal—a deadline, a successful event, or even a mutually pleasant evening—is rewarding for everyone involved. But what happens when the goal we're working toward is disingenuous?

This reward system is what manipulators prey on when they offer the victim a special opportunity. By framing the offer as rare and showing the mark that they have a lot to gain if they do what they are being asked, con artists and cult leaders whip the ventral striatum into a frenzy. Nobody wants to miss out on a potentially amazing opportunity.

The final psychological process that manipulators take advantage of involves shame. Manipulators will use shame to their advantage by triggering it in their victims. Shaming victims into giving up information, acting out against the mark's better judgment, and submitting to their will gives the manipulator the upper hand by the worst means.

Humans feel shame when we act against our own self-interest. It's an unpleasant feeling because it's meant to stop us from repeating those actions again. We feel shame when we hurt someone's feelings because it hinders our connection with them. We feel shame when we trip up on a word because it damages our projection of intelligence or put-togetherness. We feel shame when we betray someone's trust because it goes against our biological instinct to cooperate. When a bad actor uses shame against us, it doesn't simply influence the way we behave—it changes how we see ourselves.

Say, for example, you have a partner who is manipulative. After yet another night of them crashing through the door at 2 AM with no explanation or warning, you decide to confront them. *I deserve an answer,* you think, *and I'm going to get one.*

"Where have you been? And why didn't you respond to my texts at 11 PM? I was worried about you," you say, keeping your voice calm.

Instead of answering you directly, your partner spits back, "Can't I have any space around here? You're so suffocating. You always want to know every single thing I'm up to. It's not healthy."

This is where shame starts to creep in. Your cheeks burn red as your thoughts race, *I wasn't trying to be overbearing. Am I being too demanding?*

"I'm not saying I need to know everything. I was just worried. I don't sleep well when you're—"

"Oh, right, so now it's *my* fault you can't sleep? You need me here every time you want to take a nap? I have my own life. My own friends! You can't ask me to drop everything just so you can be more comfortable. That's so unfair of you to ask."

Now the shame is rolling through you, but there's some confusion too. *Being afraid of someone coming in at 2 AM doesn't seem weird . . . how did this become my fault? Is it my fault? Am I being unreasonable?*

You'd never considered yourself unreasonable before, but your partner—whom you love, trust, and feel close to—is *so* angry at you. There's no way you're totally innocent here, right? How else could this conversation take such a sharp turn?

"I was just . . . I was worried . . ."

"I'm a full-grown adult," your partner snaps. "I'm perfectly capable of coming home in one piece. I don't need you to worry about me."

Somehow, the conversation ends, and you're left feeling defeated.

Not only are you embarrassed about failing to get an answer, you're also embarrassed about wanting an answer in the first place. You thought your worrying was a normal reaction to not knowing where to find someone you love, but now it feels... invasive? Selfish? Overbearing? And you *do* share the house with your partner, and they can technically come and go as they please—what does all this say about you?

This is called gaslighting, and it's one of the most insidious forms of manipulation. A gaslighter is quick to establish trust with their victim, then use that trust to make the victim question their perception, memory, and sense of identity. Gaslighters twist words, give false information, and weaponize feelings of closeness to gain control over their victims. Once a skilled gaslighter has their hooks in you, it's almost impossible to escape because by the time you leave, you hardly know yourself anymore.

After escaping the clutches of a manipulative person, whether it's a toxic boss, a cult leader, or an emotionally abusive partner, the victim is never the same. Their ability to trust is irreversibly damaged. Their brain rewires itself to take more caution when forming connections in the future. Making independent decisions is more difficult. Rediscovering their identity is a long, complicated process that can be painful, or even traumatizing.

The average person has enough empathy to avoid using long-term manipulation tactics. We shudder at the thought of making another person agree with us out of fear, frustration, or false pretenses. Most of us recognize the widespread harm manipulation can cause. However, there will always be bad actors who want power and control more than genuine connections with others. By recognizing their most common strategies, we can protect ourselves from falling for them and stop ourselves from taking any rules out of their playbooks. After all, their tactics only offer temporary rewards, and they're followed by long-lasting consequences.

Sobering Up: When the Influence Wears Off

The problem with relying on manipulative influence—other than the obvious moral implications—is that it's fragile. It only lasts as long as the victim is unaware. Mediums can't pretend to channel the same ghost forever. Salespeople can't keep making dishonest sales pitches to the same marks. Business leaders can't maintain long-term partnerships when the initial agreement is dishonest. As soon as the trust is broken, the relationship is over, and it's unlikely to form again.

Modern-day instances of malicious influence have raised our collective guard. We're more suspicious of potentially manipulative interactions with others. No one wants to feel that cold, stinging realization that comes after falling for someone else's schemes.

Most of us can think of a time or two when we made a choice out of manipulative pressure, then regretted it later. There's a reason those moments sit so clearly in our minds: our brains take special care of memories that teach us avoidance lessons. Memories of times when we were duped, manipulated, coerced, or pressured are high-priority memories. They are prioritized during the memory consolidation process (how the brain transfers short-term memories into long-term memories) in hopes of preventing us from falling for the same trap twice.

Fear learning, or fear memory, is the strongest form of memory consolidation for the same reason: experiences that scare us are worth avoiding.[3] We're more likely to remember negative events, whether they're scary, frustrating, or otherwise upsetting. We store that interaction in an easy-to-reach place in our minds so we're less likely to experience it again.

Even a single negative interaction with a manipulator can put a person on edge for years. One high-pressure sale that ends in buyer's remorse is enough to skirt salespeople in the future. One bad relationship with an emotional abuser can cause trust issues that take years to untangle. Ex-cult members often undergo full deprogramming processes with psychology experts. Once you've experienced manipulation, even on a small scale, you're likely more aware of any attempts you come across in the future.

People are more aware (and on guard) than ever of potentially manipulative interactions. Our interconnected world makes it easier to share stories of fraudsters, which gives many of us the opportunity to avoid these interactions without ever experiencing them firsthand. Viral videos show us what to look for when they call out shady salespeople. Documentaries showcasing Ponzi schemes and multilevel marketing scams teach us to look out for similar shakedowns. Warning posts go out in communities when local business leaders take advantage of their customers.

Our growing awareness of negative influence makes it more difficult for these manipulators to function. High-pressure sales tactics are still widely used, but most people try their best to avoid pushy salespeople. The techniques might work in the moment, but they feel wrong to the person on the receiving end. And while some people willingly enter a situation where the salesperson is clearly manipulative, they proceed with caution, careful to avoid any attempts to trick them. As an example, people still visit psychics and fortune tellers, but many visitors go for entertainment. They're well equipped to resist being duped. As for manipulation in the business world, perceived trustworthiness is still a tactic that works, but unless an individual or company can demonstrate consistent trustworthiness, they lose out on customers, sales, and deals.

The more light we shed on our experiences with manipulators, the less shade they have to hide in. We can ensure we reap even better rewards by sticking to ethically sound, psychologically healthy forms of influence.

There will always be bad actors who take advantage of other people. For every person who learns how to bring out the best in others, there will be someone who learns how to bring out the worst. However, if you look closely at the ones who rely on fear, coercion, and confusion, you'll see the tiny cracks forming in their pillars of trust. It never takes long for those cracks to grow into fissures. It's only a matter of time before their whole manipulative structure comes tumbling down.

We can achieve even better outcomes by avoiding negative tactics and relying on prosocial engineering instead. By using the principles of The Upper Hand, we can ethically influence others by empowering their innate desire to cooperate instead of relying on ruses, manipulation, and coercion to get our way.

Now, if prosocial engineering is so stable, why do people even bother using negative tactics to get what they want? Why bother building a complex, harebrained scheme when you could simply ask nicely for cooperation from other people? Why pretend to be trustworthy instead of actually *being* trustworthy? The simple answer, as we'll discover in the next chapter, is that prosocial influence may be the more ethical option, but it's certainly not the easier one.

Chapter 3

OVERCOMING INFLUENCE MISCONCEPTIONS

Influencing others is easy—influencing others with only the best intentions and ethical motivations is harder. It requires you to get to know people. It requires you to tell the truth, always, even if the truth isn't what others want to hear. And sometimes, it requires you to compromise on the best possible outcome for *you* and accept the best possible outcome for *everyone*.

In the quest for successful influence, there will always be shortcut strategies that rely on manipulation, coercion, and domination. These can make The Upper Hand seem overly complicated, but that's because the shortcuts don't consider the wants, needs, and level of consent of the person being influenced.

The caveat to shorter, more ethically ambiguous strategies is that *easy* doesn't equal *right*, especially when it comes to fostering human connections. Like the glow that lures moths to a flame, these negative influence techniques often lead us astray, ultimately putting us—and the people we influence—in danger of being burned.

Influencing others with shortcut solutions creates short-term results. This doesn't always mean the influence takes less time—manipulations like long cons still take years to pull off. However, when someone sets in motion an influence strategy that relies on trickery, they also flip a proverbial hourglass. It's only a matter of time before the target discovers they've been had, and when that happens, the resulting damage is irreparable. Their trust crumbles, which causes relationships to end, deals to fall apart, and reputations to disintegrate.

Let's pretend, for this example, you're a real estate agent. A young couple hoping to buy their first home comes to you. Are you going to convince them to purchase the home that's out of their budget so you can increase your commission? Are you going to persuade them that all the extra land, extra square footage, and expensive customizations on this house are worth stretching their wallets as thin as possible, all for a bigger commission check?

It's possible, even probable, for you to convince this couple to do what you want. You can influence them to act outside their own best interest by luring them in with the sparkling countertops and manicured lawn. But what does this decision do for you in the long run?

Real estate agents rely on referrals. This couple might have friends, family members, or coworkers looking to move to the area. This one check might be huge, but if you choose to take advantage of these first-time homebuyers, you're not likely to make a lasting relationship with them. They're not going to recommend you to anyone they know, and they might even retaliate by leaving negative reviews for your firm. As first-time buyers, they're likely to sell again as their family, financial status, and relationship grow. If you take advantage of them now, they're not going to reach out to you when they're ready to sell. By using short-term strategies to secure one deal, you risk costing yourself more deals in the future.

The Upper Hand overcomes the most common flaws of traditional influence tactics by approaching interactions from the perspectives of everyone involved. This strategy for influencing others examines the long-term effects on relationships, ensuring continuous, genuine, and mutually beneficial collaboration. These techniques focus on enduring fulfillment, rather than small, fleeting victories secured through unsavory methods.

If you, the real estate agent, decide to use The Upper Hand to close your deals, you put yourself in a position for greater success. You can approach this young couple with the intention of finding them the best possible starter home, knowing the whole way that your commission depends on closing. You start by getting to know them well—one is a painter, the other is a mechanic. They're not worried about guest rooms or a large dining space, but they do want an open, airy floor plan to make their comings and goings feel more seamless.

Instead of finding them the priciest lot in the neighborhood, you focus instead on finding a home with a large garage and a space that can easily serve as a studio. You show the couple comparable homes around them, letting them weigh their options alone and making yourself available to weigh in when they want your advice. When they settle on a home, you keep them in the loop throughout the entire buying process. They're so thrilled, they leave you glowing reviews on multiple real estate sites, and every few months, they tag you as a recommendation online. The next year, you end up selling a home to their couple friends too.

To some people, prosocial influence may seem like the obvious choice when it comes to cooperating with others. However, when your prosocial influence strategies take longer, require more effort, and pay off in smaller dividends, it grows harder to walk the straight and narrow path. Little white lies seem tempting. Small sidesteps into coercion feel all too easy. This is how the misconceptions about prosocial influence form—because too often, people start out on the right path but find themselves struggling to remember the right way isn't always the easy way.

In the coming sections, we're going to address the three most common misconceptions about influence. The first concerns the addition of the word "prosocial." While influence is about getting what you want regardless of means, prosocial influence takes an ethically informed approach that ensures your strategies avoid manipulation, coercion, or other unethical forms of influence. The second misconception surrounding influence is the idea that it requires you to exude confidence or power, even if doing so doesn't reflect your most authentic self. The final misconception concerns the definition of successful influence. You might think you've succeeded if you convince the other person to strike a deal with you, but those deals don't always turn out well in the long run and may even come back to haunt you later.

These misconceptions about influence stem from the people who rely on short-term techniques. When people rely on short-term influence strategies to secure a single "yes" from others, they fail to realize how temporary that "yes" is. They only secured cooperation under the guise of the false information they provide, whether it concerns their motives, personality, or mutual success. As soon as the person they've influenced sees through them, the relationship is over.

I came across one of these flimsy influencers when I first started working in the private sector. One woman, I'll call her Diane, introduced herself to me right away. She claimed she was an ally, and she looked the part of a professional. She seemed to share my genuine passion for behavior analysis, and she was always quick to ask about my most recent projects, theories, and breakthroughs. I thought she was interested in my work... until I saw the truth.

One day, I sat in on one of Diane's presentations. I wanted to show my support for someone I thought was a friend and colleague. Imagine my surprise when her main theories looked identical to my own. I even recognized a few tidbits I'd discussed with *other* coworkers. Her presentation was a patchwork of stolen ideas.

Okay, Abbie, let's not jump to conclusions, I thought, seething nonetheless. *Science is collaborative. Maybe she simply forgot to cite you.*

Then it happened again. And again. Her work landed her promotion after promotion, despite her only skill appearing to be wrapping up other people's ideas in neat little packages. She cleverly aligned herself with the more prestigious people in the industry, and she rode their coattails up the ranks. She created flimsy relationships to secure referrals for new business. She landed public speaking roles by presenting other people's work. She went from an associate to a trainer in less than a year, all because she was charming and presented like a hard worker.

Meanwhile, I bided my time and took the slow road. I ensured every concept I claimed was entirely my own. I collaborated with others, but I made sure never to overstep their expertise or discredit their contributions. I wasn't as quick to land speaking roles or training groups as Diane, but I felt morally sound in my long-term strategy.

A few years in, Diane suggested forming a supportive think tank for some of the women in our field. I joined with a few of my colleagues. The group was meant to be an informal meeting of the minds, giving us the platform to discuss our works and potentially link up to work out some issues together. Diane also claimed it would be a bonding experience.

"Don't be surprised if we all hate each other by the end of this," she said with a laugh on that first day. "That's just what happens when you have honest conversations with each other."

The rest of us shared an uneasy look, as if to say, *Um, no, that's not my experience.* In the weeks that followed, the group devolved from a professional think tank to a reality TV aftershow. Every time one of us brought up a new idea, Diane redirected the conversation with her bile, saying things like, "It's interesting you bring that up, because just yesterday, Abbie mentioned to me that you're not even qualified in that field."

In reality, I'd simply mentioned to Diane that the idea was so prevalent in the scientific community that it was attracting the attention of researchers outside of its main discipline. Diane took my words and twisted them into an insult directed at the people I saw as friends and colleagues. And she didn't just do it to me—each of us, when presented from Diane's perspective, *did* hate each other.

After a few weeks of this "group," one of the women asked if we could talk. She told me that no one wanted to go back because of how Diane made them feel. She seemed more like a puppet master than a coach, and they were tired of her tugging on their strings. Plus, as one of them pointed out, she was clearly using the science they discussed in the group to inform her new speeches. So, the group disbanded, and none of us left with a shred of trust for Diane.

We weren't the only ones to lose taste for Diane after only a few weeks. The more I paid attention to her, the more I saw her short-term influence wear off. For example, she secured quite a few public talks, but she never secured them twice. No one asked her to return for follow-up events. She took on new clients, but once those contracts ended, she never heard from them again. She looked the part of a valued employee, but she was never invited out with anyone when the day ended. She had no relationships in the office. Any time she made a connection at work, she drained it for all it was worth, then tossed it aside.

Like anyone who relies on manipulation and false personas, Diane's resources were finite. It only took a few years for her to reach the limits of her influence. By refusing to consider how her relationships could be mutually beneficial, Diane caused people to distance themselves from her to avoid her one-sided "cooperative" proposals. People learned to keep their mouths shut when she entered a room. If Diane's name was attached to new projects, no one wanted to work on them. Her speaking engagements dried up, and no new organizations would hire her—by then, word had spread about her tendency to "borrow" ideas from other, more qualified professionals.

On her journey to success, Diane burned every bridge she crossed the moment she reached the other side. She didn't think about the consequences until she faced the edge of a cliff with no support and no way to backtrack. Meanwhile, the rest of us took longer routes to success. We learned how to build bridges together. When we reached the same cliff face, we supported each other. We crossed over and left Diane behind. If she didn't want to succeed together, we were fine with leaving her to face her mistakes.

Single-Serve Sales

There's no doubt that manipulation, coercion, and domination can be effective influence techniques. They work well for single-serve interactions where the influencer and influencee aren't expecting to interact again. However, they're detrimental for people who want ongoing relationships with others. How often do car salespeople, cold callers, or knickknack hawkers expect repeat customers? Without concern for long-term relationships, they're free to choose their influence strategy based on single interactions. However, people with long-term aspirations, like managers, executives, leaders, and teammates, can't rely on short-term tactics.

For an example of short-term success, look no further than New York City, especially around Times Square. Here, the streets are littered with street vendors selling everything under the sun: faux designer bags, "custom" artwork (purchasable in bulk), the full box set of *Law & Order* on DVD, homemade jewelry, and more. These vendors may tell you the bags are genuine, the art is handmade, and a full *Law & Order* set is impossible to find anywhere else.

These crafty vendors rely on short-term tactics to influence your decision to buy because they don't expect to ever see you again. They may trigger a sense of scarcity by recruiting another vendor to feign interest in the bag you're eyeing. They may act pushy, aggressive, or domineering to intimidate you into handing over the cash and moving along, or they may take the opposite approach and celebrate your "rare find" with you. What do they care if the vendor around the corner is selling the same item, or if the handles fall off your designer bag 10 minutes later? They have a no-refund policy. As long as you pay, they don't care how you feel about the interaction.

Short-term strategies don't care to consider how they affect their targets. They're not concerned with the effects of buyer's remorse. Whether you're buying a Fucci or agreeing to attend a business course, you'll probably have a moment of reflection once the dopamine rush wears off. You may realize you didn't actually need another bag, or that you didn't research any other courses before signing up for this one. You may even recognize in hindsight how little information the salesperson gave you before demanding a decision. Buyer's remorse doesn't feel good for anyone, and it certainly doesn't reflect well on the salesperson who caused it.

While short-term strategies have a home with the street vendors of the world, they have no place in business. In today's professional environment, most deals are pitched with the intention of collaborating for months, even years at a time. These deals require huge commitments of time, resources, and money. Before businesspeople agree to work together, they must feel like they can trust the other people involved—and if anyone stinks of manipulation, it's likely the deal will fail.

When the trust we place in others is broken, we feel betrayed. Betrayal is emotionally painful, but our brains process social and physical pain similarly.[1] The human brain responds to the pain and stores that sensation as a learning experience. It reminds us not to trust that person next time, lest we feel that pain again, and worse. The reminder also extends to people we haven't yet given trust to, but who exhibit similar traits to people who betrayed us in the past.

We're less likely to take it personally when a street vendor betrays us than when a colleague does, since we probably didn't place much trust in the street vendor in the first place. However, we probably do trust the people on our teams, so when they abuse that trust, it hurts us. When people take advantage of trust to wield influence, they cause pain for others.

If Diane had approached her colleagues with any sort of consideration for how *they* might feel about giving up their research, she might have ended up more successful today. If she'd recognized collaboration as an effective, ethical path forward, she could have joined forces with some of the best minds in the industry. She could have developed a reputation for supporting her colleagues' ideas by promoting them in her speaking engagements, courses, and media appearances. She could have built strong relationships with the other women in her field if she hadn't taken advantage of them. Now, her career is stuck at a standstill while the rest of us keep growing.

Authenticity Is the Best Advocate

People who choose manipulation, fabrication, or coercion overlook the basic human drive to seek authenticity, which is a fundamental aspect of influence. Humans crave the truth. This craving is not a conscious choice, but a result of evolutionary psychology embedded in our neural circuitry.

Inside the human brain, an intricate neural network operates below our conscious mind. It shapes our perceptions, decisions, and interactions. In the realms of influence and persuasion, the brain operates like a conductor leading an orchestra. Its processes, biases, and preferences guide our interactions as they unfold. If anyone in the orchestra chooses to stray from the conductor's guidance, the performance quickly devolves into an off-key, unconvincing cacophony.

Our brains have evolved to distinguish inauthenticity in record time. This evolution comes from an initial drive to detect incongruencies in our environment, which once helped our ancestors survive in a world where unfamiliarity meant danger. Today, this wiring prompts us to question the veracity of what we see and hear from others, making us skeptical of anyone who appears too polished or too good to be true.

Any influence approach that sidesteps openness, trust, or

authenticity is a short-term strategy. Long-term success comes to the people who decide to approach interactions with honesty—about their goals, their personalities, and their plans to succeed. Perceived authenticity goes hand in hand with perceived trustworthiness, as long as you're not authentically evil. That's why so many American political groups poll with the beer question.

The beer question is a thought experiment politicians use to determine how authentic and likable a candidate appears.[2] The question—"With which candidate would you rather have a beer?"—has nothing to do with anyone's political beliefs, platforms, or agendas. Instead, it measures the more "human" elements of a candidate, bringing them down from the political sphere and placing them in the people's favorite bar. The beer question doesn't determine which candidate is the best fit; it simply points out which is the most likable. The question reveals a deeper truth about humans—mere perception of authenticity sometimes inspires feelings of trust.

Any position that relies on a consensual power dynamic requires trust. Politicians who lose the people's trust (in theory, at least) can lose reelections. If a Realtor loses a customer's trust, they lose the sale too. A CEO who loses the board's trust will struggle to find a new position as word spreads of their betrayal. This doesn't mean the person with power has to be successful at all times—people are generally more forgiving about failure when they believe the person who failed had good intentions and tried their best. Whether they succeed or fail, the person in power must remain honest, open, and authentic.

A good friend of mine, Jay Simpson, is a celebrity photographer who exemplifies how crucial trust and mutual consent are in the professional world. Jay holds a position of power over his clients—he convinces them to become extremely vulnerable, both physically and mentally, while he snaps photos. Not only does Jay work with celebrities who are used to guarding their vulnerability from the public, he also showcases his art with big-name businesses like Calvin Klein, Nike, Target, and New York Fashion Week. He must convince his clients to be open with him, against their instincts, while both he and his clients know their collaboration will likely share this vulnerability with the world. This vulnerability is crucial, though, because it allows the photos' audience to connect with the client, therefore increasing *their* trust in the client's celebrity status.

Jay's role allows him to witness a side of these celebrities that the public almost never sees. While he collects the most beautiful moments with his camera, he also sees every moment in between, when this celebrity sheds their persona and becomes another human, one with their own self-image concerns. He must convince them to stay vulnerable despite their insecurities, even though doing so with a less ethical photographer could result in a scandal. Jay could use his position of power for selfish gains—and some people have asked him to—but it's not who he is, nor is it someone he wants to be.

Jay earns his powerful position every time he meets with a new client by staying true to himself. He exudes authenticity. Jay doesn't see his clients as celebrities, but as people with whom he'd be happy to share a drink. He doesn't enter any deals thinking about how the project could earn him cash or fame; he sees his projects as a collaboration between artist and subject, and strategizes the best way to meet both people's goals.

His mission is to keep his clients comfortable, despite the high-pressure nature of his work. Jay must convince every client to step out of their comfort zone. He needs them to be vulnerable with their bodies so their honest emotions come through in the photos. Whether they're showing humility, power, confidence, sadness,

OVERCOMING INFLUENCE MISCONCEPTIONS

happiness, or any combination of emotion, they have to *feel* it to show it, and they can't feel anything but discomfort if Jay doesn't lay the groundwork.

In 2006, Jay landed his first meeting with an A-list celebrity. The client's agency set the meeting in an empty conference room near their office. Jay arrived first and sat down in a gray chair, at a gray table, looking at the gray walls. He started unpacking his belongings, but after a few moments, he stopped.

This is awful, he thought, watching the gray clock tick gray seconds away. (The second hand was red, but the seconds *felt* gray, you know?) Jay felt stifled here, like he was about to pitch an insurance plan instead of an art project. *There's no way he'll listen to me like this.*

When the celebrity arrived, Jay greeted him warmly but didn't sit back down. Before they dove into business, Jay moved toward the door.

"Do you want to go get some coffee? It's stuffy here. Let's find a more comfortable place to talk."

"Sure," the client said with a smile, "that sounds lovely. I know a great place right down the street."

Jay wanted out of the gray conference room because it didn't allow him space to be himself. He wasn't a businessman—he was an artist, and he felt stifled in a conference room. Now, in a bustling coffee shop full of sights, sounds, colors, and space, he felt more authentic. Instead of sitting next to each other at a comically large conference table, the two could sit across from each other directly, like two friends.

Since then, Jay's never taken any special considerations for his celebrity clients. Part of what makes Jay so appealing to his Hollywood clients is how little he cares about their stardom. In fact, he often goes out of his way to *ignore* any recent news about them, whether it's true or not.

"Every time I meet someone new, I like to meet them on a human-to-human level," Jay told me. "I don't want to know who they married or divorced or how long they were in rehab or what awards they won. I want to know how their day is going."

When Jay enters a business relationship with a client, he ignores whatever power dynamics existed before and balances out their relationship by getting to know the person, not the persona. He wants to work together to make the best possible piece of art. Once his client expresses the same goal, it doesn't matter who's more famous. All that matters is that they both succeed.

The trust built between Jay and his clients lasts long after the photoshoots are finished. Since his trustworthiness is authentic, his business interactions often evolve into the beginning of friendships. He always gives clients his personal phone number, and he encourages them to reach out for any reason. Sometimes they do, and other times he reaches out to them—he's the type of guy who remembers birthdays and anniversaries, and he's quick to send off a celebratory text. When he travels for a shoot, Jay reaches out to old clients in the area, always willing to catch up over a cup of coffee.

While Jay's connections certainly help his business, that's not the reason he connects with people. He genuinely cares about the people he meets. He values the trust he builds with them. His clients recognize his trustworthiness, authenticity, and professionalism, so they refer him to *their* friends, who meet him and connect with him just as quickly. Jay's business thrives *because* he uses prosocial influence with his clients. It's not a skill he developed as an afterthought to a successful business; it's how he built his success in the first place.

Jay's mindset differs from other business owners who rely on short-term strategies to success. Other photographers see their clients as simple subjects, as valuable to the shoot as a bowl of fruit. These photographers enter deals thinking, "What can this subject do for me?" instead of a more collaborative, balanced mindset of, "What can we do together?" While self-serving photographers might see spikes of success when a photo goes viral, Jay is the one building a slow, steady, stable reputation in his industry.

Business practices like the ones Jay employs demonstrate what it looks like to secure The Upper Hand. Lasting influence that yields long-term success needs trust. Trust not only makes for a more ethical exchange but ensures the people on both sides of an interaction feel comfortable and confident in their decision-making process. The "yes" we secure from using The Upper Hand is genuine, because both parties' goals and expectations are aligned.

But what happens when a business's practices aren't designed with trustworthiness in mind? What results can we expect from situations that are engineered to pressure the "yes" instead of securing it through ethical, considerate means? If you're looking for proof that unethical influence is most likely to go wrong, you can find it by simply turning on your TV.

Swimming with Sharks

ABC's *Shark Tank* is an American reality show that relies on some of the most high-pressure influence tactics out there. The premise of the show puts insane pressure on the contestants by itself—landing a spot on an international TV series has serious implications for the business owners—and the influence techniques employed by the show only make the experience more stressful, ultimately creating an environment rife with unethical influence.

Each season, thousands of entrepreneurs compete to present their product to high-profile investors on *Shark Tank* in hopes of securing a business deal. They must make pitches compelling enough to convince the sharks—the investors, who are fierce, frenzied, and predatory—to make an offer on the spot. There are other versions of this show around the world, as well as similar series like *Lion's Den Finland* and the Canadian *Dragons' Den*.

Across the United States, business owners look to this show to guide them through interactions in which they seek to influence investors. They falsely believe that when they see a shark make a deal with a business owner, they're watching successful influence in action. In reality, they're watching a high-pressure situation in which coercive strategies actually influence the contestants, not the sharks.

The business owners who make pitches on *Shark Tank* and its sister shows feel so much pressure to secure a "yes" from the sharks, they don't realize how the deal hurts them long term. This pressure comes from the people at home who support them, the sharks they look up to, and even the producers of the show, who warn entrepreneurs that if they don't accept a deal, their segment isn't likely to make the episode's final cut. If an offer comes, the pressure to accept, negotiate, or decline can be overwhelming for the small-time entrepreneurs, and limits their critical thinking skills. They might say "yes" in the moment, but it doesn't take long for the regret to sink in.

Now, if *Shark Tank* isn't an environment where entrepreneurs thrive, why is the show still running? How did some of the products, like Bombas socks, Scrub Daddy sponges, and Comfy wearable blankets, end up wildly successful? Why do business owners still compete to pitch their products? The answer is simple: while the deals often fall apart in the real world, they make great TV.

Shark Tank's process makes engaging television because it's dramatic. The thumping, *Jaws*-like theme song, the moody lights, and the temperamental sharks keep viewers enthralled. The more people watch, the more exposure businesses gain, so business owners jump at the chance to be featured, which often means accepting a deal whether it's in their best interest or not.

Behind the camera, though, *Shark Tank* resorts to some negative influence techniques to maintain that TV-grade drama. The whole interaction is socially engineered to be stressful. From their first step on set, entrepreneurs enter "the tank" via a long hallway walled with screens showing real sharks circling them. This creates an immersive experience that makes entrepreneurs feel like they're entering the sharks' lair, increasing cortisol levels and adding more stress to the situation.

When the entrepreneurs reach the main stage, they see the "sharks" seated in lush chairs on a raised platform. This immediately secures the divide between predator and prey, as well as a "them versus me" mentality. Once entrepreneurs begin their pitch, it's not uncommon for sharks to interrupt them, talk over each other, or outright dismiss the deal before the pitch is over. The influence tactics at work on *Shark Tank* can be so overwhelming, some entrepreneurs buckle under the pressure. One contestant actually fainted on the stage in the middle of his pitch. Since then, the show has kept a psychiatrist on hand, and all entrepreneurs meet with them right after finishing their pitch.[3] The environment isn't collaborative; it's combative.

Compound the pressure of an unfamiliar experience with the pressure to make a deal, and you have the perfect recipe for regretful business decisions. Most of these entrepreneurs aren't used to being on television. Even if they've had some experience filming commercials, the *Shark Tank* environment is undoubtedly less comfortable. The bright stage lights, glinting cameras, and all the backstage crew members' gazes can be downright overwhelming. Nothing about this environment is comfortable for the entrepreneur by design. It's what gives the show its stakes.

In the real world, business deals rarely function how *Shark Tank* makes them appear—in fact, not even the deals made on *Shark Tank* function the way they appear. Plenty of the show's featured businesspeople walk away with a handshake deal, but many experience severe buyer's remorse when their stress levels out. They realize, once they're no longer starstruck or stage-frightened, that giving away half their business for a measly $100,000 wasn't the best decision. They realize how much they were influenced by the show and feel embarrassed, distraught, and, sometimes, angry.

These emotions don't bode well for the beginning of a long-term partnership, so it's not uncommon for *Shark Tank* deals to fall through after filming is done. Only about 27 percent of the deals featured in the show's first seven seasons actually closed.[4] Sometimes the sharks pull out of the deal, too, after looking deeper into the entrepreneur's hard data. They know as well as the entrepreneurs do that if they enter a deal feeling lied to, taken advantage of, or reluctant to move forward, the deal is dead in the water.

The majority of successful business deals come out of environments designed for comfort, confidence, and critical thought. Shortcut solutions work every once in a while, but for every Scrub Daddy success story, there are dozens of stories like the ShowNo Towel, You Smell Soap, and Hy-Conn. When people are placed in high-stress, coercive situations, they might say yes, but the "yes" doesn't last.

OVERCOMING INFLUENCE MISCONCEPTIONS

Influence techniques can be useful during negotiations, but those negotiations only produce long-term success when they're based in trust. High-pressure influence tactics lead people to get carried away by the short-term solution, distracting them from the negative consequences looming just out of their foresight.

Using scenarios like the ones presented in investment shows like *Shark Tank* will cause business owners to engage in unethical influence. They can result in breaches of trust, missed business opportunities, or worse, a total collapse of the company. Environments built to foster high-pressure decisions, coercion, or manipulation only make it harder to secure The Upper Hand.

A Glowing Reputation

Today, relying on influence tactics that only secure short-term wins isn't just a bad business plan—it can ruin careers. Word travels fast in our digital age. Online reviews are a massive consideration for growing companies. If you're known for your cutthroat negotiation skills or your manipulative business dealings, you'll struggle to secure any business, new or old.

If your reputation precedes you, make sure it's a good one. Every time you give in to the temptation of shortsighted influence tactics, you risk your reputation. One little slip here and there isn't likely to ruin you, but even the smallest deviation into the world of unethical influence could cause you to be "canceled" if the world at large uncovers your tricks. People don't appreciate being used, manipulated, or conned, and if they feel like you're guilty, they're quick to denounce you.

In the case of Diane, she believed her unethical influence only mattered on a case-by-case basis. By the time her errors caught up to her, it was too late to change, and her business suffered as a result. She earned a reputation for disingenuousness, and it will likely follow her for the remainder of her career.

Compare her story with Jay, who built a prominent photography career thanks to his consistent authenticity, reliability, and openness. Jay has established such a reliable reputation, he has the luxury of choosing the people with whom he collaborates. He bases his decisions on whether he feels the same trust and authenticity he extends to others, since their projects are the ones he finds most rewarding.

In the business world, maintaining a trustworthy and ethical reputation is crucial for long-term success. People who prioritize mutual consent, authenticity, and transparency in their dealings tend to build lasting relationships based on mutual respect and shared goals. These qualities not only maintain existing relationships but also help you attract valuable partnerships through your positive reputation. By consistently demonstrating ethical behavior, you can distinguish yourself from others in your industry and earn the respect of your peers, colleagues, and clients alike.

Creating, sharing, and engaging in authentic interactions with others is the best way to secure The Upper Hand. When you ensure you've considered the perspective of the person you'd like to influence, you guarantee the relationship grows out of a mutual desire to succeed. The more meaningful relationships you foster this way, the more opportunities you'll have to build a strong reputation. Your presence online and in person is bound to grow alongside the relationships you nurture. Prosocially motivated people shine bright enough for everyone to see, and their light attracts other people who value honest, ethical interactions as well.

Part II

USING INFLUENCE

Chapter 4

GETTING A GRIP ON THE UPPER HAND

Many of us have seen people with a natural talent for influence. These people are so charming, commanding, and eloquent, they seem to have a hold on an entire room the moment they walk in. While it may be confounding or even annoying to see these talented influencers at work, with the right knowledge, anyone can appear just as gifted once they sharpen their persuasion skills.

The Upper Hand is the toolkit for graduating from influencer to master. The Upper Hand takes the innate abilities most—if not all—human beings have; considers their biological, social, and psychological makeup; and uses science to build predictable, ethical, and consistently successful techniques that will get you a "yes" that lasts long after you leave the other person's presence.

As we've seen, using conventional influence techniques can secure an immediate "yes." But it often leaves the person you've influenced feeling disconcerted, with a sense that something is "off."

Then, when the person has time away from your influence to think about the offer, your persuasion usually doesn't last. I was reminded of how tenuous these immediate "yeses" can be when someone tried to use these techniques on me.

In 2023, I was invited to speak on a panel for an annual cybersecurity conference. This event focuses on changes, updates, and strategies for protection in the cybersecurity industry. It was a great opportunity, and the fact that it was hosted in Barcelona made it even more tempting.

The panel discussion went well, and afterward I was milling about with my own colleagues and attendees when a well-dressed man approached me. He looked to be in his mid-thirties. He introduced himself as Dylan.

"Dr. Abbie," Dylan said, "I just wanted to say that I loved your comments today."

"Thank you," I said. He seemed pleasant enough, but he was leaning toward me in a way that suggested he was about to ask for a favor.

"You know," he continued, "I've just started a cybersecurity company, and I was wondering if you had any advice on securing grants. I took note of your strong academic background."

I acknowledged with a "mmhmm."

"I mean, you do behavior analysis, *and* you have a PhD in psychology? Really incredible CV. I'm pretty blown away!"

I felt the tingle of alarm bells in the back of my brain. I don't mind compliments, but something felt off. What was he after?

"Thank you," I said curtly.

"Well, I'll have to gather my thoughts on what sorts of support my team could use on the grants... Can we set up a call to talk further? I know you're probably busy for the rest of the conference."

"Um," I looked around for Areesa, who manages my consulting work. I couldn't spot her in the crowd. I sensed if I said no, I'd be stuck in this conversation for longer. A "yes" was probably the quickest way to get rid of him. "Yeah, sure."

We exchanged contact details. At least the next time we met, it would be through a computer screen, and Areesa would be there to talk about consulting fees.

The day of the meeting approached, and Dylan asked to adjust the time. Areesa couldn't make the new time. I was already a bit uncomfortable, and I considered canceling. But if I could secure a lucrative consulting contract, it would benefit not only me but the whole company.

I logged on to the meeting, and after we exchanged generic pleasantries, I listened while Dylan spent 20 minutes explaining his situation: how he got started, what his company does, and how fast it's growing. He told me most of the company's positions were filled now, but he still needed to find a CEO. He needed to raise capital while he searched for someone to fill that role. Some of his business partners were on a board of directors for another company, and instead of consulting for current grant proposals, Dylan wanted me to pitch to this other company on his behalf.

"I can just see you now," he said, "stood up on a stage, representing our brand. I researched you earlier today, and I know these guys are gonna love the blend of psychology, cyber security, and your OSINT expertise... They might toss a check or two right up onstage with you. You really are the perfect fit."

Again, a flash of... nerves? Anger? It was becoming clear to me he didn't really research my background or expertise that closely—I'm not an open-source intelligence (OSINT) expert as he mentioned.

"Well," I said, "here's what I can do. I'll connect you with Areesa, who can discuss details of consulting. I charge an hourly fee for my consulting work, and I specialize in the human side of security. I do not carry out OSINT. In the meantime, I noticed you don't have a human security sector for your business—let me put you in touch with Chris, our CEO. He can help you there."

"Great, Abbie. Thanks so much, and I'll speak with you again soon."

A few hours after the meeting, I had enough time to process the interaction. I considered the red and green flags that appeared to me in hindsight after our meeting. I considered our first in-person meeting as well.

Some interactions give us "gut feelings" that are easy to dismiss. However, if we dissect our reactions from a biological, psychological, and sociological perspective—biopsychosocial, for short—we can see how gut feelings are a result of larger, more complex reactions. Every "sense" is a signal from the brain and body, and if we understand which senses we trigger in others in an interaction, we can be more ethical and effective persuaders. We need to avoid triggering negative, stress-stimulating senses, and instead trigger positive feelings that allow for critical thought and genuine connection.

The first red flag came when Dylan rescheduled our meeting, excluding Areesa. Areesa keeps track of my availability, public presence, and level of interest with new opportunities—and she often measures it faster than I do myself. For me, a meeting on the details of my public speaking without Areesa is like a movie screening in a language I don't speak.

With this change in social dynamics, I experienced a psychological and biological change too. I felt less mentally prepared, which changed my emotional state from one of cautious optimism to nervous anticipation. My body registered the psychological change, and instead of seeking a reward, it switched on my threat avoidance mechanisms. I grew uncomfortable.

The red flag during the virtual meeting was more subtle, but it concerned *how* Dylan praised me. All his "compliments" reduced me to my physical appearance. In fact, he admitted he "saw" me as the perfect fit for his company before he ever saw my credentials. He wasn't interested in what I would say to investors once I was up on a stage. Well, I'm not a spokesperson, nor am I a company mascot—I'm a scientist, and a doctor at that.

The discomfort I felt rising throughout that interaction came from my unconscious mind processing all these little jabs at once. While I consciously focused on him talking—and boy, did he have plenty to say—my unconscious mind processed massive amounts of information, parsing out the hidden messages in his words. This meant more cortisol, which meant more anxiety. My body and my unconscious mind wanted me out of the situation as soon as possible.

When I suggested Dylan meet with Chris, I thought I'd done so genuinely, but I realized in hindsight I had deeper motivations. First, I wanted off that call. Second, I trusted Chris to give me his honest take after meeting Dylan, and I hoped it would align with mine. Somewhere in my mind, I knew to reach out to Chris to validate my "gut feeling." I filled in Chris that Dylan would be coming his way, and caught Areesa up on the potential consulting work.

Strangely enough, Dylan's "ask" got bigger when he spoke with Chris, despite having no rapport with him. Chris debriefed me after the call and shared that Dylan had tried to poach me from Social-Engineer to work for his cybersecurity startup as the acting CEO, a role I neither wanted nor was qualified for. When Chris questioned why he wanted me, let's just say there was no mention of anything skills-based, but instead talk of how "sex sells" and he needed a young woman to make the company look appealing to investors. Chris and I had a good laugh, and when Dylan followed up with me, I cut all contact with him.

Dylan may have been good at persuading investors, professionals, and experts to meet with him, yet I sensed his influence likely wore off once he wasn't face-to-face—or screen-to-screen—with the person he was trying to influence. Sure, he successfully secured initial "yeses." But after that, with time to consider his offer, I suspected others, like me, backed out.

When people like Dylan use traditional techniques to influence, they often leave the other party uncomfortable, even consciously skeptical. Dylan likely didn't realize the effect his flimsy influence tactics, not to mention clear disregard for ethics, had. He ignored my expertise in favor of my appearance. He ignored my current position in favor of what he wanted for me. He ignored my comfort and confidence during the interaction in favor of his own. If he was really serious about hiring me, his attempts to do so didn't make me want to maintain a continuous working relationship.

The Upper Hand framework provides a deeper understanding of how influence works during an interaction. Analyzing any interaction from a biopsychosocial perspective can be beneficial, but it's crucial for interactions based around making deals—particularly deals with high stakes and long-term implications.

Influence works best when it builds from an understanding of human biopsychosocial reactions. Ignoring how the body, mind, and social climate relate to an influence attempt is a surefire way to crash and burn. To truly gain The Upper Hand, we need every component functioning well, giving us a firm grip on the interaction.

GETTING A GRIP ON THE UPPER HAND

Understanding How The Upper Hand Works

There are five key principles to consider before making a play for The Upper Hand in every interaction. Each principle considers how to address the psychological drives occurring in every human brain. When you successfully wield The Upper Hand, you address the most important psychological drives motivating critical interactions. Since the brain is such a complex system, made up of interconnected parts, these drives can be conscious or subconscious, depending on which part of the brain processes them.

These drives come from the three parts of the brain we've developed over thousands of years of evolution—the old, the middle, and the new. The old part of the brain deals with survival issues, like breathing, eating, drinking, and staying warm and safe enough to stay alive. This part of the brain is often colloquially called the reptilian brain, or the crocodile brain, because like crocodiles, it is most concerned with basic survival needs.

The middle brain handles our emotions. The middle brain is also responsible for our social skills, and feels joy and pain from social situations. The middle brain sends signals to our body about how we're feeling. When a friend rejects our ideas for dinner plans, the little hurt we might feel is sent by the middle brain.

The new brain, the most recently developed in evolutionary history, takes care of logic, critical thought, and complex information processing. These newest parts (which are still about 1.5 million years old[1]) are often called the executive functioning center, and it includes parts like the neocortex. The executive functioning parts of the brain make it possible for us to have emotional responses and resist acting on them.

The Upper Hand framework takes the old, middle, and new parts of the brain into consideration and accounts for the underlying psychological components that affect everyone involved in each interaction.

Each principle of The Upper Hand is mapped to a digit of the human hand. Like our fingers, each principle can function alone in specific interactions, but they are most powerful when they're understood together, serving as a holistic guide to using influence effectively.

We Are Our Brains: The Thumb

An opposable thumb is a unique trait that separates humans from other species in the animal kingdom. Thumbs are required for precise gripping, holding, and grabbing objects. It's how we evolved to make and use tools, and some evolutionary scientists believe that once our precise grip evolved, humans only learned to walk on two feet because our hands were busy.[2] The thumb is also the only digit that can easily touch all the others, which makes it the perfect digit to encapsulate this first principle.

The human brain is the most obvious trait separating us from other species. There is nothing on the planet with the kind of efficient processing power resting between our ears. There's a reason supercomputers and processors are so often compared to the human brain—the structure of computers was informed and inspired by an understanding of the human brain's neural network. Consider how complex a supercomputer is, then multiply that by a thousand—that's how intricate, powerful, and complex our brains are.

We aren't simply creatures with brains—we *are* our brains. Yes, we have heads, shoulders, knees, and toes, but our brains allow us to have thoughts and control our bodies instead of being ruled by external stimuli. To understand ourselves and others, we must understand how our brains work on a mechanical level. Ignoring the brain's role as the driver of every decision a person makes is like ignoring our thumbs' role in the simple task of picking up an object.

The human brain is powerful, but it also requires massive amounts of energy to keep it running smoothly. The brain only makes up about 2 percent of our body's overall mass, but it takes up around 20 percent of our body's energy.[3] Just as supercomputers need massive amounts of energy to process information, so, too, do our brains.

Because our brains require so much energy, they are prone to conserving energy wherever they can. One method brains use to save energy is to send information down well-worn neural pathways instead of forging new ones, resulting in some cognitive shortcuts. Thinking critically—that is, using the executive functioning power of our brain—is highly taxing. This is why we might break out the calculator to do fairly easy mental math, and have trouble changing habits and long-standing emotional reactions. It's not impossible to change our behavior, but it takes far less energy to carry on with existing behavior.

When we set out to influence someone, we must first understand the brain is in charge. Cognitive functions, biases, and drives all contribute to a person's choices, whether or not the individual is conscious of it. Tapping into this understanding helps us assess interactions from an informed position, ultimately maintaining a stronger, more effective grip with The Upper Hand.

The Drive to Survive: The Index Finger

If you are reading this sentence, it is because every single one of your ancestors, since the beginning of time, successfully passed down a brain built for surviving. Their instincts, drives, and tendencies helped them accomplish the ultimate biological drive: they passed down their genes and perpetuated the cycle of evolution.

When the brain processes new information, whether it's an obvious visual threat or a complex social situation, its first determination is how this information impacts our immediate survival. Sometimes this evaluation takes place in our conscious minds—like when we look down over a steep ledge or see a bear off in the distance—but most of the time, we're not aware of how often our brains are checking our survival odds.

Survival drives stimulate the fight-flight-freeze response. When the amygdala, the part of the brain that processes emotions, receives threatening information, it sends a distress signal out. This signal is received by the hypothalamus, which then communicates to the rest of the brain to trigger fight-or-flight mode. This response floods the body with stress hormones like cortisol and adrenaline, which provides a physical advantage in the upcoming interaction.

The fight-or-flight response affects almost every part of the body. The heart beats faster to increase blood supply for running or fighting. Small airways open wider to increase oxygen intake, giving the brain a higher level of alertness. Glucose moves from temporary storage inside the body to transfer energy quickly. The entire body remains on red alert until it receives a new signal from the hypothalamus that the threat is gone, defeated, or neutralized.

The survival response, like all psychological drives, has its pros and cons. The brain's survival procedures help us leap out of the way of a moving car before we're even aware of the danger, which makes them useful. However, since the survival response comes from the oldest part of our brains, it's not adept at differentiating between the threats our ancestors faced and the psychological and social ones we face today. The brain enacts the same response to a snarling lion as it does to a pushy salesperson. The context of the response is irrelevant to influence strategies—the existence of the response is what matters.

Sometimes, people trigger the survival drive to coerce others. While this can get a "yes" in the immediate term, it doesn't lead to lasting influence. The car salesperson might be able to coerce one sale from an individual, but it's unlikely they'll be able to get the second sale from that same individual. Buying a car was stressful with that salesperson! It's not an interaction most people will want to repeat.

Since survival is a priority in any given situation, it is often a barrier in successful influence. To gain The Upper Hand, we must avoid triggering the survival drive. Otherwise, the brain will be distracted trying to neutralize the threat, rather than thinking about making a decision. If you want someone to be cooperative, you must first make them feel safe.

The brain can't focus on decision-making during an interaction if it perceives an imminent threat. It will instead be guided by the drive to survive, which can be difficult to predict, making influence harder. To encourage cooperation and long-term "yeses," influencers must avoid triggering the drive to survive. (More on how to do this in the coming chapters.)

We can think of the survival drive as the index finger of The Upper Hand: it's useful in many contexts, and while it sometimes gets in the way—have you ever accidentally hammered your index finger instead of a nail? It's not fun—there is no doubting how useful it is. Both the index finger and our survival instincts are great at pointing out danger, although neither are always adept at helping us escape it. However, when using influence, making a point to accommodate the human survival drive is sure to help you gain The Upper Hand.

Connect and Cooperate: The Middle Finger

"Giving the finger"—presenting only the middle finger on the hand toward someone or something—is a sign of disrespect in many Western countries. However, this middle digit, when thrown up, can help foster *or* fend off one of our most persistent drives: to connect and cooperate with others.

In 1968, a US Navy ship named the USS *Pueblo* was captured by North Korea. While the US government struggled to find a way to get their men back, North Korean officials built a propaganda campaign around them. They released photos and films of their captives, claiming they were treating the men with the utmost respect. What these officials didn't realize, thanks to the nonverbal language barrier between Americans and North Koreans, was that in every shot, the Navy men were displaying exactly how they felt about their imprisonment by flipping their middle fingers to the camera.

"It helped us survive and kept morale up," said one of the crewmembers during an interview years later. "For that little period of time, we were in charge of our own lives."[4]

These men were held captive for almost a year, and during that time, throwing up their middle fingers in a small rebellion was a key part of their survival. It helped them connect with each other and communicate their true feelings to the outside world. On one hand, the gesture worked as a prank—when North Korean officers noticed, the men claimed they were flashing a "good luck" gesture. On the other hand, they shared a crucial message with the world: "don't let their propaganda fool you; we are prisoners here."

While the brain is wired to survive, it is also wired to make connections with others. Some people will argue that survival is more important than connecting with other humans—after all, another person could kill us. However, research isn't so clear-cut on this.

Humans have evolved as a social species. Our brains are wired to seek out connection with each other, and we are rewarded with a cocktail of feel-good neurotransmitters when our search pays off. It would be easy to assume we only seek out connections to mate and pass on our genes, but the drive to connect with others appears in the brain long before a human is capable of reproducing.

Making connections with others—parents, siblings, friends, strangers—is how humans have survived for millennia. Humans are one of the only animals on Earth born completely helpless. A human infant can't walk, find food, or protect itself from danger for *several years*. For a baby to avoid starvation, dehydration, or any other thousand ways to die, they must rely on other humans to care for them while they continue to develop outside of the womb.

The more our ancestors grouped and built communities, the more often they survived the dangers of their times. The drive to survive and the drive to connect and cooperate grew to be intertwined—as modern humans, we are dependent on our "tribe" to meet both needs.

As a baby grows into an adolescent, they still rely on other people for support. They might be smart enough to remember where and when the wild trees bear fruit, but not strong enough to raise shelter or hunt for animals alone. Thousands of years ago, it was easier to take down an angry elephant with a group of humans. Today, it's easier to face losing a job, receiving a hard diagnosis, or months of imprisonment in a strange country with a support system.

The Upper Hand framework taps this powerful drive to connect and cooperate. Additionally, the most skilled social engineers also wield humans' innate social drives. Being connected and cooperating with others makes us feel safe. When a person feels socially safe, their brain gets a rush of the neurotransmitter oxytocin.

Oxytocin is often known as "the love hormone" or "the cuddle hormone," but it's perhaps better understood as the "social trust" hormone.[5] We don't only receive oxytocin from hugging, kissing, and skin-to-skin contact—we receive oxytocin when we hold eye contact with others, sing in unison, or see others perform a good deed for another person. Oxytocin feels good—it's how our brains reward us for securing connection with others, which ultimately benefits our chances for survival.

The drive to survive is largely driven by cortisol, the main stress hormone, whereas the drives to connect and cooperate are ruled by our instinct to seek oxytocin. Instead of making the person we're trying to influence stressed out to force a decision that benefits us, we can trigger their desire to connect and cooperate, motivating them to make a decision that is mutually beneficial.

Understanding how the drive to connect and cooperate works is crucial for successfully wielding The Upper Hand. The desire to connect and cooperate is just as strong as the survival drive—it just operates in a different way.

Of course, there are other factors that can make attempts to connect more likely.

Mind-Body Feedback Loop: The Ring Finger

The ring finger got its name because it's the finger for promise rings, engagement rings, and wedding bands. An old belief claims that the ancient Egyptians popularized this finger as the ring finger because of its connection to the heart; they believed there was a vein in the ring finger that ran directly to the heart. We eventually discovered that wasn't true, but the symbolism stuck around—the ring finger still symbolizes the connection between mind (love) and body (heart).

Our brains constantly collect internal and external information, process it, and respond to it. Signals come and go from the brain, either requesting action or responding to information. If we feel physically cold, our brains send a series of signals to make us throw on a jacket. Once we do, our brain receives signals that help it determine whether we're comfortable or if we need another layer. This is the mind-body feedback loop—a constant cyclical process between mind and body.

Understanding the mind-body feedback loop in our brains contextualizes common emotional and physical cues. This loop doesn't have as much of a sway on a person's choices as their survival odds or their drive to cooperate, but it's still a factor worth considering. It can tip the odds of successful persuasion in your favor.

Most of us know how torturous it is to sit through a business meeting on an empty stomach. You end up more interested in the ticking clock than the presentation in front of you. Your stomach lets out thunderous rumbles every few seconds, and when someone mentions the "stakeholders," you start daydreaming about a juicy ribeye. Until you satisfy your hunger, you can't think clearly. You might even have trouble controlling your temper because you're subconsciously or consciously focused on your next meal.

While hunger is an easy signal to read, there are some subtler physical signals we struggle to decipher. Many emotions evoke similar sets of physiological symptoms, which isn't a problem most of the time, since emotions are regulated by the middle, less conscious part of our brains. However, when we're asked to consciously label our emotional state, we often misattribute one emotion to another.

For example, one study examined the misattribution of arousal, which refers to the tendency to confuse fear with sexual attraction.[6] Experimenters asked a group of men to cross two bridges: one was sturdy and short, the other tall and rickety. After the men crossed a bridge, a woman who asked them questions from a seemingly unrelated survey stopped them. She gave each man her phone number and told them to call if they had any questions or comments about her survey.

Most men who crossed the rickety bridge gave the woman a call. Meanwhile, the men who met her after crossing the stable bridge weren't as moved by the woman's presence. Why? Well, when the rickety bridge group encountered the woman, their hearts were racing, their breathing was short, and their hands were shaking. What could be the cause if not this polite woman asking them questions?

Of course, it was the bridge that made the difference. The adrenaline the men felt after crossing a fear-inducing bridge felt, to them, like a sign of attraction when they met this woman. The men who crossed the stable bridge didn't have any physical sensations of arousal, so they were less likely to call the woman after the encounter.

The idea that our minds and bodies influence each other is known as embodied cognition. Physical states inform our impressions, which can affect our decisions. However, the mind-body connection exists outside of our conscious awareness most of the time, so we're not always aware of how our physical environment weighs on our mental states.

We can find examples of embodied cognition in everyday language. Our experiences in the physical world influence our cognition and are reflected in how we express ourselves. Expressions like "my heart is broken," "I'm in over my head," and "it hurts to think about" are all physical descriptions we use to express sensations.

One of the most powerful examples of embodied cognition is the relationship between physical and social warmth. When babies' brains form their first neural pathways concerning warmth, there is a connection between the physical and social sensation. The warm, physical feeling of a mother's womb before birth and a mother's warm skin after birth is entangled with the social sensations of caring, nurturing, and loving. As babies grow, the neural pathway strengthens, and the connection between the two sensations grows stronger as well.

It's hard to imagine that an act as simple as holding a warm drink could influence how warmly you perceive a new person, but it's true.[7] The connection works in the opposite direction too—meeting someone we perceive as "warm" and kind can make us feel physically warmer. Along the same lines, feeling physically cold can influence how detached, unfeeling, or "cold" we perceive a new person.

Knowledge of the mind-body connection and embodied cognition help us effectively wield The Upper Hand. Making a meeting room as comfortable as possible helps eliminate mind-body connection factors that could distract or dissuade people. Comfortable temperatures, seating options, and even food and drink choices are just a few of the factors that could help you maintain an edge during an interaction.

Self-Identity: The Pinky Finger

The final principle of The Upper Hand may seem like a smaller consideration when compared to the larger principles like survival and connection, but it's still a crucial component to ensuring successful influence. This principle is all about the drive to maintain self-identity. This applies both to your sense of self—your beliefs, morals, and values—and the self-identity of the other party. Believe it or not, people are less willing to cooperate with you if you bring their sense of self into question.

Each of us lives with a set of biases that make up how we see other people, ourselves, and our place in the world. Whether we like it or not, every interaction we experience shapes our reality and either builds or strengthens our biases. This is a normal part of brain function—biases come from our brains creating mental shortcuts to better process information. Without knowing it, we form stereotypes, judgments, and assumptions about other people, places, and belief systems. These biases then dictate our behaviors.

Biases may be conscious or subconscious. They need not be positive nor negative, but they can be harmful. Unconscious biases can lead people to discriminate against others without cause. For example, a male hiring manager with gender bias may overlook a female candidate, influenced by a subconscious bias that male candidates are better suited to executive roles. The man may not recognize the gender bias in himself—he simply feels the male candidate is a "better fit."

When a person feels their identity is under attack, they often experience a stress response. If someone's identity is strongly tied to their job, and then they are laid off, they may feel extra stress in being untethered from their self-image. Similarly, if we disparage or question a person's self-perception while also trying to persuade them, our attempts to influence are unlikely to succeed.

On the flip side, if we can resonate with someone's self-identity and connect with it, our messages become more appealing to the other party. Brands attempt to influence consumers to purchase their products and services by appealing to common values. Celebrities gain and lose followers when they speak passionately about their political views. And social media apps keep us scrolling by showing us more of the content we "like"—which is usually content that appeals to our self-identity.

People are driven to preserve their self-identity as they move through the world, and sometimes this drive is more important to them than the truth. When self-identity is questioned, confronted, or contradicted, it's uncomfortable. People often avoid, undermine, or dismiss notions that invite inconsistency into their perceived reality ... which isn't an ideal outcome for an influence attempt.

The human brain struggles to hold on to two conflicting, similarly valued beliefs—this struggle is known as cognitive dissonance. Decisions about which belief to choose are made in the newest parts of our brains. Maybe we'll evolve to build broader subjective realities that can account for contradicting ideas, but until then, we're more likely to enter fight-or-flight mode than rationally accept a challenge to our most valuable beliefs.

A person's self-identity can affect how cooperative they want to be, how safe they feel, and how willing they are to make a deal with you. If you appeal to a person's self-identity, you're more likely to create a connection. If you infringe on a person's self-identity, your chances of influencing them decrease, especially if they find your infringement offensive to who they are.

Self-identity is relative; what is a compliment to one person's self-identity may be an insult to another. When Dylan first approached me about grant writing and my academic background, I was interested in a possible collaboration. But when it became clear he wanted me more as a salesperson with no real autonomy or power, I lost interest. Instead of appealing to my expertise, Dylan appealed to skills unrelated to what I consider most important to who I am.

Rather than attempting to influence someone to *think* differently (for which they'd have to change their self-perception), it's much more effective to show them how working with you falls in line with their existing self-identity, beliefs, and values. If Dylan had led with sincere respect for my true expertise (behavioral science, not OSINT), perhaps we'd be working together.

Entwining Principles with Practice

These five biopsychosocial principles address the underlying drives of all human decision-making. This knowledge is paramount to wielding The Upper Hand. The coming five practices—Create a Tribe, Speak Their Language, Pants Yourself, Shelve It, and Hold, Don't Squeeze—are *how* we'll take the five principles and put them into action in our influential interactions.

In the next section of the book, we'll cover these five practices. We'll review how each practice considers the principles we've covered in this chapter, the "digits" of The Upper Hand, and uses them to inform approaches to influence. Each practice takes you through all the considerations you can make in your interactions to increase your odds of securing the "yes."

In the next few chapters, we'll explore how the knowledge of human decision-making informs the five practices of The Upper Hand framework. While it's tempting to view the next sections as a sort of playbook for influence, The Upper Hand is not a one-size-fits-all guide. Following its practices won't guarantee flawless influence attempts. Additionally, there is no set order in which you must use these practices. Some of them may not even apply in every interaction. While The Upper Hand may not act as a step-by-step instruction manual, it *does* act as a toolkit you can use to grow into a master influencer.

The reality of the human experience is that we're all different. Each person brings their own experiences, biases, and interpretations to every interaction. The best influence strategies start with The Upper Hand as a foundation, then rely on you to adapt in the moment as you learn more information. In essence, The Upper Hand is a guide, and it's meant to help you reach your ultimate goal: effective, ethical, long-lasting influence.

Chapter 5

CREATE A TRIBE

It's your first day as manager at a new company. How are you going to convince your new team to trust you, respect you, and cooperate with you? Old-school tactics might advise you to establish a power dynamic, reminding your new teammates who's boss. When you want something done, you don't ask, you demand. You don't earn respect—you command it from your subordinates.

These old lessons in leadership come from the very beginning of human social groups. About 300,000 years ago, early humans created tribes around strong, dominant leaders. These leaders were typically the most dominant "alpha" males. They ensured the group's survival by protecting against predators so the others could focus on gathering food and securing shelter. The first social groups in recorded history only had about 10 to 15 members, but as time went on and these groups merged, their respective leaders clashed.

When two or more nomadic groups of humans collided, their leaders took on a conquer-or-be-conquered mentality. Brute force and violence resulted in a surrender or a murder, and the winner took the leadership role. As humans established permanent homes and stopped roaming as much, tribal leaders gained influence through conquest, raids, pillages, and war. Dominance reigned, and only the most aggressive tribes survived.

It wasn't until the civilizations that would eventually become ancient Rome and Greece formed that leadership grew to include more than forceful survival. These cultures were the first to consider leaders who valued education, rational thought, and the pursuit of knowledge. Ancient philosopher Aristotle posited that the best leaders were the ones who pursued virtues and led with reason, not raw aggression.

The popularity of ideological leaders grew, especially among humans with more brains than brawn. People became more motivated by a shared system of beliefs rather than a collective fear of challenging authority. However, it didn't take long (about 100 years) for advantageous people to dominate this form of leadership, turning idea-driven societies into dictatorships. This was the era of Hitler, Stalin, Mussolini, and Mao.[1] Instead of dominating through straightforward public violence, they influenced their followings through fear, treachery, and manipulation.

While dictators throughout history collected power at alarming rates, it was always short term. They did nothing to reduce the amount of human suffering within their tribes. They established regimes based in fear, not trust. They dominated instead of cooperating, and many people fled from them as a result. These subjects risked punishment, persecution, and death, all to break free from such a flawed leadership style. The subjects who didn't choose flight eventually chose to fight, and they enacted violent evictions on these oppressive leaders.

Domineering leadership might work for kings, dictators, and

CREATE A TRIBE

tyrants with armies behind them, but only for short periods of time. Since our days as small, nomadic tribes led by brutish alphas, we've learned more about human behavior, relationships, and motivations. If you choose to lead your new team like an authoritarian ruler, you inspire mutiny, not cooperation.

The best way to get what you want from others is to inspire connection (and thereby trust). The most successful influencers inspire others to believe what they say, value their advice, and accept their influence. Once you've made it clear you're not out to get anyone, you can gain better results by offering tempting choices.

It's not typically easy to build trust with total strangers, but you can reduce the odds of triggering their stress response to make them feel, if not bonded, at least safe. Before you can think about convincing your team members to work with you, you must convince them to talk to you in the first place. It's easier to influence people with whom you've already established a positive relationship. Striking up chitchat with a friend or colleague you already know feels natural, which makes transitioning to influence feel natural. These people feel connected to you, and they trust you not to lead them astray. It's more difficult to influence a stranger, even when you have some form of power over them.

As the new manager at a company, you might decide the best way to make a good first impression is to make yourself available. Instead of shutting yourself in your new office as a show of force, you decide to take a walk around the office. You see your new team members busy at work. You smile and nod as you pass by, but one desk catches your eye, and you stop for a closer look. There is a framed picture on the desk of a family posing in front of the Grand Canyon.

"Wow, what a great picture," you say to the young man at the desk. "I was just there last year. Isn't it beautiful?"

"Oh, yeah!" he says. "That's from our trip a few years ago. It was one of the best trips we've taken. The kids loved it."

"I can see by those big smiles! How old are they now? What are their names?"

You spend another few minutes chatting with the young man—you learn his name is Marco, that he's head of logistics—before continuing your stroll. You stop at another desk to comment on the football logo on Marketing Mike's desktop background; it's your favorite team too (and it actually is)! A few desks over, you and Sarah from accounting discover you both worked for the same company 10 years back. You learn from Jamie over in sales that the team goes out for drinks on Thursdays, and that managers are always welcomed to join.

Before lunch, you realize you've met every member of your new team without holding a single meeting. A group of them invites you to a local restaurant, where you learn even more about one another. They talk about their work, what they're excited about, and what they're dreading. After lunch, Jamie pulls you aside.

"We're really excited to have you here," she says. "You seem like a great fit. The whole team loves you already."

By the time you hold your first official team meeting a few weeks later, it's clear you've established a baseline of trust. The team might not accept your new initiatives with enthusiasm, but they hear you out and ask thoughtful questions. They ask your opinion on strategies they've used for years before you joined. The whole team works together, and there's a clear path to success by the time the meeting ends.

What you've done here is utilize the first practice of The Upper Hand: Create a Tribe. Crafting a sense of unity and community, a "tribe," around some commonality establishes an initial bond with

CREATE A TRIBE

another person. These bonds are quick and easy to form around simple things, such as shared interests, physical attributes, and experiences, from long lines in the grocery store to vacation destinations to former workplaces.

People often create a tribe when they strike up conversations with others. A customer at the cafe might notice the barista is wearing a Pittsburgh Steelers button on their apron and make a comment about the most recent game. You might strike up a conversation with a person who's wearing the same watch as you, asking them what prompted the purchase. You might share a wry laugh about forgetting to bring a book to read in the long line at a grocery store. Creating a tribe positions you as a nonthreatening member of the same team.

Starting an interaction with a shared interest creates a sense of familiarity. Typically, we humans are on the alert when confronted with strangers. By finding something to connect over, we put others and ourselves at ease—we feel psychologically safer, if only slightly.

Finding a shared interest with another person (or people) triggers an oxytocin release for everyone involved. This hormone counters the stress hormone cortisol and primes us for a more positive social experience. The more we connect, the more oxytocin we trigger (in ourselves and others), and the safer we feel.

Creating a tribe is like a warmup for your interaction. In fact, most "icebreaker" prompts used in the corporate world are designed for people on a team to create a tribe together. It seems simple enough when you think about it—people bond better when they have something in common—but too often, people ignore this practice, diving straight into a pitch. Like any warmup exercise, whether it's in the office, the gym, or a local hangout, choosing to skip this first practice can make gaining The Upper Hand more difficult.

Think for a moment about a recent interaction you've shared with a stranger—how did it start? It's doubtful that a stranger approached you and said, "Hello, I'd like to start a conversation with you." Instead, it's more likely you and the stranger connected over something you have in common. Maybe you said, "cool shirt," because their shirt depicts a band you like, or, "How do you know James?" because you met at James' retirement party. You may have even commented on the recent weather. (This is sort of a last grasp at connection, but hey, I'm British, so it's my go-to small talk!)

To successfully wield The Upper Hand, you must allow the other person to feel safe. Creating a tribe with them is a way to align yourselves as allies, signaling that you're not a threat nor an obstacle to their well-being. It's a way to indirectly say, "Hey, fellow human, we're in this together." Once the two of you feel united under the same banner, you're in a much better position to practice your influence skills. Their calm, safe state allows them the space to think critically about your eventual offer, making it more likely for you to secure an enthusiastic "yes."

Why It Works: Utilizing the Principles of The Upper Hand

When it comes to influence, it's good to keep in mind the three C's: comfort, confidence, and competence. When meeting someone new, you'll want them to feel comfortable speaking with you, confident in their role in the conversation, and competent enough to fulfill their role in a collaboration. Maintaining a safe environment is a precursor to comfort, just as comfort is a precursor to confidence and competence.

CREATE A TRIBE

As humans, we're more likely to cooperate with others when we see them as members of the same tribe or social group. We feel more comfortable, confident, and competent within our tribes. We're not just emotionally motivated to support other tribe members—we're biologically motivated too. The Create a Tribe practice shows us how to leverage what we have in common with others to appeal to the survival drive—the pointer finger principle of The Upper Hand.

Whether our tribe is made up of primitive hunter-gatherers or modern football fanatics, our brains know there is strength in numbers. By associating with other people who share ideas, goals, and interests with us, we feel more secure in our environment. It's not always easy to tell whether another person is a threat to us, but when we find a commonality, we find familiarity, which makes us feel safe.

Creating a tribe also utilizes our innate drive to connect and cooperate, the middle finger principle of The Upper Hand. It's not enough to simply stand in the same room as others to see them as part of our tribe. We must forge a connection by finding out what we have in common.

In England, there are few tribes stronger than the ones formed around a favorite football (soccer) team. On any given Saturday during the Premier League season, one could step into any pub in England and find groups of fans dripping in memorabilia from their favorite team, watching the game on the dozens of TVs around them. When their team scores, the fans share their enthusiasm with hugs, claps on the back, and cheers heard from streets away. When their teams lose, they share their grief too. But does their camaraderie extend beyond what happens on the field?

In 2005, a classic study set out to determine how far these English football fan tribes extended when taken out of a sports-based context.[2] Scientists designed experiments to test two long-standing rival teams' fans—Liverpool Football Club and Manchester United. These two teams have shared a rivalry since the 1980s, and their fans are known to hate each other. Each teams' fans have a rival chant about the others, and it's not uncommon for fights to break out following a Liverpool vs. Manchester game.

The experiment took 45 male, self-identified Manchester United fans and exposed them to an incident where another person—a stranger—tripped and fell about 15 feet away from the subject. The stranger, yelling in pain and gripping his ankle, had on either a Manchester shirt, a Liverpool shirt, or a plain, unbranded shirt. The goal was to measure whether the original Manchester fan, once he noticed the stranger, would intervene. They were ranked on a scale of 1 through 5, where 1 meant the subject never saw the stranger fall, and 5 meant the subject went out of his way to help the stranger up, then escorted him for further assistance.

Out of the 35 valid participants (10 were removed for not noticing the stranger at all), a pattern emerged: 12 out of 13 Manchester fans were rescued—that's over 90 percent! However, only 33 percent, or four out of 12, plain-shirt strangers received the same help. The number of Liverpool fans saved was even smaller at only three out of 10 (30 percent).

The experimenters theorized that while the participants weren't *less* likely to help Liverpool fans, they appeared *more* likely to help their fellow Manchester fans. In other words, their responses were more likely positive (recognizing a commonality) than negative (choosing to ignore based on difference).

The experimenters ran the test again with new participants, but with one slight change. This time, the participants were primed to think of themselves not as Manchester fans, but as football fans in general. This new category expanded their perceived social group

CREATE A TRIBE

to *include* Liverpool fans. As expected, the number of participants who helped up the fallen Liverpool fans grew significantly (from 30 percent to 70 percent) while the number for plain-shirted strangers dropped even lower (from 33 percent to 22 percent.)

The results of this experiment indicate we're wired to respond better to what we find familiar. In an emergency situation, our brains work on an unconscious level to seek similarities—members of our tribe—before we put ourselves at risk by offering help. Even the smallest form of tribal identification, like a familiar T-shirt logo, can influence how we respond to others in our environment.

It's crucial to note that we're not only inclined to respond more efficiently to the familiar; we also respond *less* efficiently to the *un*familiar. When we enter situations we find unfamiliar, our stress response is triggered. Cortisol levels rise to help us spot danger, escape routes, and weak points lurking in our surroundings. This stress response might have been advantageous when exploring a new, wild territory, but it's less helpful when entering a potential customer's boardroom for the first time. Similarly, when we invite business partners to our familiar environment, their stress response may impact their presence.

Creating a tribe limits the brain's responses to the unknown during an interaction. By aligning ourselves with the other people, we wave a bright banner around the room and use it to represent our shared values, interests, and goals. We unite underneath this banner, which bolsters us to accomplish more together.

How to Create a Tribe

Mastering the skill of connecting over commonalities requires some subtlety. This strategy isn't simply about offering up your favorite hobbies and interests to see if your interaction partner shares them with you. It's about actively eliciting information from your interaction partner to determine what *their* interests are, then offering up ways they connect with your own. If you try to fake, force, or fabricate a connection, you slip into the sphere of manipulation, and you risk breaking trust. However, if you come on too strong, you risk appearing pushy or manipulative, which decreases your odds of forming genuine connections and trust.

Creating a tribe requires you to highlight commonalities without appearing opportunistic. By drawing attention to what you and another person have in common, you open a door to your tribe for them to step through. How successful you are at inviting them through depends on *how* you open the door: how wide you swing it, how long you leave it open, and how inviting you make the space on the other side.

There are variations of the Create a Tribe practice. You can choose whichever suits your influence strategy best. Creating a tribe between you and one other person is the most obvious choice. However, sometimes creating a tribe with another person and purposely excluding others from joining triggers the parts of our brains excited by exclusivity, which can be more valuable in certain situations. Finally, you can create a tribe with multiple members at once, which is a trickier task to accomplish, but can merit strong results if done well.

Creating a tribe with another person requires more than a compliment—it's about pointing out what aligns you and your interaction partner best. Sometimes the initial effort to create a tribe *does* resemble a compliment, but it must go deeper than that.

Say you're looking to practice creating a tribe with a potential customer, a man named John. "That's a nice suit," is a compliment. "That's a nice suit. I've been looking for a local tailor to make my suits fit better. Who do you use?" is a *connection* point. You and John are similar because you both have interest in tailored suits—not simply suits off the rack. You compliment John's style, and, with more context, it's clear to John you have a genuine interest in the suit beyond pure flattery. Validating John's appearance, then asking him for a recommendation is an opportunity for the two of you to connect. You're clearly two people who value a well-fitted suit—what else do you have in common?

It's likely you and John share even more commonalities, perhaps a preference for cotton over tweed, or a favorite local cocktail bar. The more you and John connect over your commonalities, the more you can find: maybe you both live in the same city, you enjoy the same types of movies, or you have similar ideas for future business endeavors. You now have an opportunity to band together under a bespoke banner, all because you reached out and established a connection.

If the other potential sellers in the room are also wearing well-tailored ensembles, you might need a more customized approach to create a tribe with John. Creating a tribe between *only* two people is most effective in scenarios where you want the other person to feel a special connection with *only* you. In this case, John may appreciate the chance to offer tailoring recommendations, but it's also possible some of the other suits will chime in with *their* recommendations, strengthening the connection with the whole room, but weakening any potential bond between only you and John. Then your one-on-one conversation devolves into a group discourse around double-breasted blazers, and you lose your advantage with your potential customer.

Instead of commenting on John's suit, you can pivot to find a connection that only applies to the two of you in this situation. Here are a few rapid-fire examples:

If you and John are the first to arrive at the meeting, you can create a tribe around valuing timeliness. "If you're not early, you're late, am I right?"

If you and John meet by the coffee pot, you can create a tribe around your coffee preferences: "There's a great coffee shop down on Main. Have you ever been? Their dark roast is unmatched."

If you and John appear to have absolutely nothing in common except the same quality of suit, you can make small talk until you find something to relate about: How was his drive in? (Does he drive a similar car to you?) How was his weekend? (Does he spend his weekends on the same activities as you?) Is he local, and how long has he lived here? (Are there any local spots the two of you can share stories about?)

Eventually, it's almost guaranteed you and John can form a tribe. In fact, if you practice this strategy with every person in the room, you're bound to form a tribe with almost everyone individually, or as a group, just like the new boss in this chapter's opening story. Humans have more in common with each other than we think, and creating a tribe is all about finding one commonality that both people find interesting, valuable, or unique. Doing so helps ebb the cortisol we sometimes feel when meeting someone new.

Creating a tribe on a larger scale can be as simple as uniting a group under a single, simple banner for a short period of time. The best speakers open their talks with experiences or stories the audience can relate to. Coaches unite their players around a shared team identity and team objectives. Flight attendants bring together entire planes of people from different cultures, classes, and contexts by uniting them around the one thing they all have in common: wanting a safe flight to their destination.

If you're looking to create a tribe with a team before pitching a tough project, the best way to do so is by offering a shared experience right at the start. Bring in some breakfast for everyone and allow opportunities to bond over bagel preferences. Better yet, bring the team to a restaurant and create conversation around menu options. The more you share with your team, the more opportunities you have to align with them personally and professionally.

Creating a tribe around shared interests like favorite foods, hobbies, or past experiences lays a strong foundation for collaboration. Interactions that foster connection on a personal level allow trust and camaraderie to grow, which leads to more opportunities for successful influence. As long as your efforts to connect with others are genuine, they can serve as powerful tools for beginning to gain trust and utilizing The Upper Hand.

Finding Balance: Calibrating for Connection

Successfully creating a tribe with another person requires you to strike a balance between offering a compliment, creating a connection, and passing judgment. If your attempt at creating a tribe is too subtle, the other person may simply think you're offering a polite compliment, and the conversation skids to a stop with a small "thanks." On the flipside, if you come on too strong, they may overlook your attempt to bond and instead consider your comment judgmental, which essentially ruins your chance to influence them.

Compliments alone, when they're sincere, aren't tools for influence. The only goal of a sincere compliment is to let someone know you admire them, whether it's for their outfit, their personality, or a choice they've made. Compliments rarely open the door to a conversation on their own. In some cases, a compliment can lead to a tribe-creation opportunity, but if that's your goal when offering a compliment, the compliment isn't sincere anymore.

Be mindful of the kinds of compliments you offer. Complimenting someone's appearance may seem like an easy start, but you never know how someone else feels about themselves, especially not right away. One man's "doe eyes" are another man's "beady bugeyes," and you don't make quick progress by accidentally pointing out a person's sensitivity. That's not to say you should never compliment someone's appearance—it's simply a riskier move to compliment someone's complexion than it is to compliment their T-shirt.

If you offer a sincere compliment to someone with whom you'd like to create a tribe, follow it up with a connection opportunity. This doesn't diminish the genuineness of your compliment; instead, it expands your compliment into a conversation. Most of the time, a simple expansion around *why* you admire this particular trait enough to compliment it is opportunity enough. However, be careful using this approach, since clumsy wording may accidentally tip the connection scales out of your favor.

Sometimes, compliments + context + delivery ≠ connection. Miscommunications and misinterpretations always have the potential to throw off your influence equations. When this happens, sincerity can appear as passive aggression, or even judgment. While this may not be your intention, if your interaction partner feels even slightly threatened, your window for influence starts sliding closed. Better to add more context than not enough.

Like Goldilocks, we want to find a strategy for creating a tribe that feels just right, making sure our interaction partners feel valued, interested, and comfortable.

Too subtle: "I like your T-shirt." *Oh, thanks.*

Too harsh: "I like your T-shirt. I always want to wear a nice band

CREATE A TRIBE

tee, but I'm always afraid I'll feel underdressed." *Um . . . does that mean you think I'm underdressed right now?*

Just right: "I like your T-shirt. That band is one of my favorites—what did you think of their last album?" *Oh, thanks! I thought it was pretty good, but it's a pretty big step away from their old music. What about you?*

Striking a balance between offering compliments, building connections, and avoiding judgment is crucial to creating tribes with others. The door you open when you invite others to share a tribe with you must be as welcoming as possible. Meaningful connections create opportunities to align others both personally and professionally, paving the way for successful influence.

Once you've got the other person on your side of the threshold, you can strengthen the bonds between you with the next practice of The Upper Hand, which covers deeper connection opportunities over shared goals, values, and beliefs.

Chapter 6

SPEAK THEIR LANGUAGE

Creating a tribe with a stranger is a great first step to make them feel safe with you. However, if you want to increase your power to influence, you need a stronger connection. If creating a tribe is how we invite someone through an open door to an interaction, speaking their language is how we make them feel comfortable inside.

When I say this practice of The Upper Hand is "Speak Their Language," I'm not suggesting you learn a new language. Instead, focus on sharing a common context in your conversations. Find out what's important to the other person, then build a sort of "shop talk" around your shared beliefs, values, and goals. By doing so, you show the person you'd like to influence you're someone with whom they can connect, communicate, and collaborate.

Showing people we speak their language means carefully crafting how we reflect back what they consider respectful, meaningful, or trustworthy. Speaking someone's language can be as simple as holding back curse words around your politically correct grandmother, or repeating industry-specific terms when discussing a friend's job. I love when people come up to me after a speech and say things like, "Your talk was amazing!" But if someone approaches me with, "Your speech got me thinking... what are your thoughts on the underlying neurological mechanisms responsible for embodied cognition?" I light up like the Rockefeller Christmas tree.

Years back, I applied for a lectureship position at Northampton University in the United Kingdom. I wanted the position with all my heart, so I put all my time and energy into practicing for the interview. It wasn't enough for my resume to match their job description; every candidate would meet most, if not all, of their qualifications. If I wanted to stand out, I had to show them more. I couldn't present as the perfect candidate for a university lecturer—I needed to present as the perfect candidate for a Northampton lecturer. When I entered that interview space, I needed to show the hiring team how well I spoke Northampton's language.

This interview took place during the COVID-19 pandemic, so the meeting was virtual. Without the in-person advantage, my influence strategy was limited. Still, I did the best I could with what I had. I made sure the background visible in the video call portrayed professionalism (as best as it could from a university dormitory room). I dressed for success from top to bottom, not only to present well on camera, but to make myself feel more confident and capable. I made sure I had a warm cup of tea on hand to soothe my nerves.

By the time the interviewers signed on, I was as prepared as I could be. I knew all their names, specific fields of study, and most recent publications. I could practically picture myself on the other end of this interaction in the future.

I greeted each interviewer personally, then the interview began in earnest. As we went forward, my anxious energy converted into excitement. I knew the answers to their questions. I had memorized mottoes, acronyms, and ideal subject matters for the school. By the time the more specific questions came, I felt more comfortable than ever.

"What do you consider your ideal lecturing environment?"

I had taken special preparations for this question. At the time, Northampton University was in the process of swapping out large lecture theaters in favor of smaller, more intimate halls. A recent finding at the school discovered that smaller groups helped facilitate more independent learning and were more accommodating for neurodiverse students and staff.

"I thrive in small groups as opposed to grand lecture halls," I said. "I find that smaller groups feel more connected and give students more chances to communicate with me and with each other. I know large spaces have their benefits in some cases, but overall, I find smaller halls to be more rewarding for everyone."

"I see," said another interviewer, marking up her notepad. I watched her circle something a few times.

"So," the first interviewer continued, "if you were to fill this position, how do you think your research will fit in with the university's greater collection?"

"That's a great question," I said, "and I have a few ideas already. I noticed that Professor Halt is currently researching age-related cognitive decline, which would be an interesting collaboration with my work on nonverbal communication skills. I also think a collaborative effort between the clinical team working on complex trauma and my work examining the life histories of serial killers could bring in some valuable work for the university."

As I spoke, I watched another interviewer's eyebrows raise as he considered my response. I could see his pen scratch a short note at the bottom of the screen. I waited patiently for him to set his pen back down.

"You have clearly done your research, Ms. Maroño," he said briefly.

The interview continued for a while longer. The interviewers left me with a line that wasn't a "yes," but wasn't a "no" either.

"Regardless of the outcome," one had said, "I am sure you are someone we would love the opportunity to collaborate with."

As I closed the screen of my laptop, I was terrified and nervous. But I was also satisfied I had done all I could. I knew I was unlikely to be the best candidate based only on my written credentials, but I was confident I had shown my passion for this school, at this time, with this staff. I had put in the time and the effort to find what makes Northampton unique and how I would fit.

There is power in communication, whether it's verbal or nonverbal. By adjusting how you present yourself to best complement what the other person finds familiar, appropriate, and comfortable, you immediately give yourself The Upper Hand during your interaction. Your effort to speak their language inhibits any stress response they may have, and it also sets up an unconscious desire to connect with you.

Sharing a language with someone else doesn't require you to be dishonest or inauthentic. It doesn't require any unethical practices. During my interview, I didn't lie or make anything up. I didn't embellish my qualifications, nor did I pretend my knowledge was some stroke of luck or coincidence. I wanted my interviewers to know how much I prepared. I wanted them to take notice of our shared language, not only as academics, but as people who were passionate about Northampton.

If you try to speak someone's language from an inauthentic

SPEAK THEIR LANGUAGE

position, you're more likely to make a fool of yourself than make a new connection. Take Joey Tribbiani from the TV show *Friends*, for example.[1] Joey is a lot of things—he's sweet, he's kind, he's charming—but he isn't very intelligent. When his best friends need a recommendation letter for an adoption agency, they don't initially ask for his help.

"We don't think of you as really being so much . . . with the words," Monica says.

Joey wants to prove them wrong, so he sets out to write the most intelligent letter he's ever written. Instead of learning "big words" to help make a genuine case for his friends' adoption request, he opts for the thesaurus option on his computer. He swells up with pride when he presents the final draft . . . totally unaware that what he's written doesn't make any sense.

"They are humid, prepossessing homo sapiens with full-sized aortic pumps," Chandler reads out from the letter.

"And hey, I really mean it, dude," Joey replies, beaming.

"Joey, I don't think we can use this," Monica says. "You signed it 'Baby Kangaroo Tribbiani!'"

By trying to be someone he's not, Joey accidentally embarrasses himself (or would have, if he was smart enough to understand his mistake) and puts his friends' adoption efforts at risk. He only resolves his mistake by delivering a new, meaningful, authentic letter directly to the adoption agency. Monica and Chandler panic at first . . . until the adoption agency calls them geniuses! By securing a letter from a child, they demonstrated how well the couple speaks the same language as him—they guessed little Joey must be eight or nine, based on his drawings!

When I interviewed for the lecturer position, I didn't try to be someone I'm not. I simply showcased the parts of myself that would best fit the university's mold. That doesn't mean the other parts of me were hidden; I didn't hide my lack of lecturing experience or my missing certifications. Instead, I showcased my willingness to learn and earn.

We all speak many languages, sometimes on a daily basis. The way we interact with our families differs from how we interact with our coworkers. We greet our friends differently than we greet strangers at checkout counters. The jokes we tell our partners might not translate well in polite company, but that doesn't stop us from cackling in the privacy of our own homes. We adjust and adapt to keep ourselves and the people around us comfortable. It's part of being human.

We put more conscious effort into sharing a language when we put together job applications. We've all taken job descriptions and matched some of the language with our qualifications on paper. Tailoring a resume and cover letter with keywords you believe will catch the hiring team's attention isn't dishonest; it's just good job-hunting.

There's nothing wrong with bringing someone's attention to your most complimentary traits. As long as you aren't hiding your authentic self in the process, you can maintain honest, inviting interactions this way. The university lecturers wanted to know about my qualifications for the job, so I spoke the educators' language. It's not the language I'd use with my dad, my best friend, or the barista at my local coffee shop. But it was the best fit for this particular interaction, and it undoubtedly influenced the eventual job offer I received from Northampton.

Why It Works: The Comfort of Commonalities

When you're a stranger in a strange land, your brain goes into high alert. You stay on the verge of a full fight-or-flight response, constantly scanning for any threats to your survival. You could be all alone or surrounded by people, but if you can't communicate effectively with them, they do nothing to ease your nerves. They might even make you more nervous. But recognizing the sound of your own language sends out a signal of potential safety, and your brain urges you to follow that voice!

Whether you're lost in the Peruvian jungle or acting as a sole company representative at a convention, finding someone who speaks your language motivates you to connect with them, and vice versa. It's a strength-in-numbers instinct. That initial connection grows as you two uncover shared beliefs, histories, and aspirations. The more you relate, the stronger your desire to collaborate becomes.

We're considering The Upper Hand's thumb and pinky for this practice: We Are Our Brains and Self-Identity Protection. To speak someone else's language, we must recognize the cognitive functions and biases that impact how others move through the world. Once we have a basic understanding of a person's worldview, we can use that information to influence our approach. Then, we can form a stronger connection, which increases the odds for successful influence.

People will likely have a hard time communicating with someone who literally doesn't speak their language, but so, too, is it difficult to communicate with someone who speaks a language of different values and morals. We (and our brains) like to confirm and validate our existing beliefs, and we gravitate toward people and groups who facilitate this. We're more likely to be convinced of messaging when it comes from someone in our in-group.

The tendency to seek out what confirms or strengthens our worldview is called confirmation bias, and it applies to information as well as connections. Conflicting information, especially when it applies to our worldview, is psychologically distressing. The brain would much rather reinforce (and seek reasons to reinforce) existing neural pathways than challenge them or break them down. As powerful and adaptive as they are, brains want to conserve energy, and deviating from existing neural pathways to create new ones is energy heavy.

Familiarity is psychologically safer than its opposite. When we speak someone's language, we suggest a familiarity with what they hold sacred. We set their minds at ease by assuring them we're not a threat to their worldview. We make them feel comfortable by validating their self-identity, or at least validating their desire to keep it intact. We make them want to work with us because we assign ourselves to the same in-group, the same team, which helps the other person feel their self-identity is safe.

Each of us has a sense of who we are, however blurry that sense may be. In sociology, the concept of the self and self-identity is separate; the self (the essence of a person) is a mental concept of who a person is across contexts, built from social relationships and socializations. Self-identity is separated because sociologists believe each person has multiple identities to use in different social settings. For example, you might have one self-identity you use with your friends and another you show in the workplace. The clothes you wear, the jokes you make, and the tasks you take on are probably different in each setting.

Our self-identities are built out from our perceptions, beliefs, and values concerning the world around us. The three main components of our sense of self are how we value ourselves, how capable we feel, and how much control we have over our own lives.[2] Our values around loyalty, creativity, and compassion may be strong across all identities, but manifest differently depending on the setting. The one piece all our identities have in common is how valuable they are to us.

My work is a massive part of all my identities. I consider myself a scientist above all else. Whether I'm actively working or hanging out with my friends, my identity as a scientist saturates my sense of self. I've said it before in this chapter and I'll undoubtedly say it again before the book is through—the best way to get me going is to ask a question about psychology. You start speaking my language with science, and I'll keep talking until you stop me.

Since my professional passions are always at the forefront of my identity, I'm also quick to recognize people who try to influence me without appealing to my identity. And if someone either accidentally or purposefully insults my role as a scientist, it's almost guaranteed I'll never willingly collaborate with them. My worldview is shaped by science, and if I can't share it, I can't share myself.

On the flip side, speaking the same language also means knowing when to hold back, resisting the urge to challenge another person's worldview. I struggle with this myself when I speak to people who don't believe in evolution, because I am a staunch believer in the overwhelming scientific evidence supporting evolution. However, I have had a few occasions where I worked with creationists. In these situations, if the topic arises, I don't blindly agree, as that would be disingenuous of me, but I also don't verbally attack the person in front of me. Doing so would only put them on the defensive, which does nothing to make either of us feel valid. Instead, I do not bring up the topic unless directly asked. When asked, I simply present the science, citing the peer-reviewed text and evidence that have influenced my knowledge.

Remember, the brain is more comfortable validating its

currently held beliefs. If you try to change someone's entire moral code over a cup of coffee, the coffee might end up all over your clothes. You don't have to agree with someone on every concept to connect and collaborate, or to influence them. You must simply share a basic understanding that as long as your conflicting ethical values don't affect your shared goal, you still have an opportunity to work together.

When you set out to speak someone's language, you must tread carefully. Hold back from making an attempt until you're comfortable with the amount of information you know about them. If someone mentions their kids, don't assume their whole identity is being a parent. If someone brings up their favorite politician, make a note not to trample on their opinions, but don't write them off as an extremist. If what they say is intriguing to you, speak their language by asking about it. If it's not interesting to you, or you sense you won't agree, don't follow that thread of information. As long as you stay respectful, authentic, and cooperative, there will be other parts of their self-identity you can connect with authentically.

Speaking their language allows people to identify as part of the same in-group. And when two people feel they are part of the same in-group, they are more likely to be receptive to one another. In a business environment, setting aside time to speak the same language as potential partners, customers, and stakeholders increases the odds of them feeling connected to you, which improves your odds of success. Cold calls, sales, and negotiations can be tough because they don't utilize any sort of identity sharing (or if they do it's often disingenuous). But when you present yourself as a trustworthy face in a sea of strangers, your influence job becomes easier.

SPEAK THEIR LANGUAGE

How to Investigate, Validate, Relate

We can break down how to speak someone's language into three parts: investigate, validate, and relate. When I interviewed with Northampton, I did much of the investigation before the meeting started. Then it was fairly easy to validate and relate during the interview. However, with strangers, or when meeting with new people, you'll likely have to spend a bit more time investigating before you can validate and relate—a.k.a. speak their language.

Let's break down an instance of one entrepreneur using this tactic to eventually secure a pitch meeting.

Two businessmen, we'll call them Freud and Darwin, are seated next to each other at a networking event in New York City. Freud is an entrepreneur looking to secure funding for his next project. Darwin is a venture capitalist hoping to invest in emerging tech. While the two wait for the day's events to begin, Freud turns toward Darwin and strikes up a conversation.

"Beautiful morning, isn't it?" he says, nodding toward the sunlight streaming through the tall windows behind them.

"Yes, it is," says Darwin.

Freud follows up: "Are you here visiting, or are you a New York local? Your accent suggests you're not from around here."

"Indeed," says Darwin, "I moved here several years ago. It's a little crowded, but at least the park is quieter this time of year, and there's not as many gray days as in London."

"Oh, wow. I love London—I lived there for a time. Beautiful city. Great pubs."

"I do miss a pub. They're not the same here. Too posh." Darwin pauses and studies Freud. "So, what brings you to the conference, then?"

"Oh, you know, same as most people—looking to connect with other entrepreneurs and funders. What about you?"

"Ah, go on then," Darwin says, raising his eyebrows. "Don't hold back now, let me hear about your big idea."

"Oh, well," Freud replies, "it wouldn't be fair of me to blab on about myself until I hear what sorts of ideas you invest in."

Darwin gives a bemused look. He explains succinctly that his fund is interested in lifesaving tech.

"Oh, like medical devices, or bio-hacking breakthroughs, or ...?" Freud queries.

"Any of those and more, I guess," Darwin says with a shrug. "Whatever has a good chance of saving lives."

"Huh," Freud says. His big idea is a gaming app for adults with addiction. The clinical trials showed promising results, but they need investors to run a bigger trial and help lobby support from health insurance companies. But before he reveals this, Freud wants to know more about Darwin's self-identity and worldview, his "language."

"That's very noble of you," Freud says. "Can I ask why or how you got into that area? Most of the VCs I've met so far are more concerned with numbers and returns. Not that I blame them. That's important too."

"Well, of course," Darwin says. "We can't fund anyone if we don't have any funds to begin with. But as to your question about how I got into the field..." Darwin then explains a personal experience that inspired him to follow his passions and invest in lifesaving tech. Freud nods along, paying sharp attention to the information Darwin shares.

The lights in the auditorium flash twice, signaling the session is about to begin.

"That's really cool," Freud acknowledges. "Looks like we're about

SPEAK THEIR LANGUAGE

to start here—but, if it's amenable to you, I'd love to grab lunch and talk further, or set aside time to pitch to your firm. In short, I'm building tech to help addicts recover. And now that I have some more information on what sorts of ideas you're investing in, I think it could be worthwhile to talk."

"Doesn't sound like a bad idea," Darwin hedges.

"You know," Freud sighs, as the lights dim and the crowd around them quiets, "saving lives is pretty important to me and my company too."

"Alright, yeah. Let's talk," Darwin agrees.

Let's break down this conversation, specifically Freud's line of questioning. The two men went from total strangers to potential business partners in the span of a few minutes. First, Freud took a swing at creating a tribe by pointing out the nice weather. It didn't work to crack open the conversation, so he followed up with another common question that could draw the two into a tribe: Where are you from? When Darwin revealed a new detail—that he previously lived in London—Freud was able to connect to that piece of information.

Note: Freud could have picked up a thread of conversation regarding New York City, and there's no saying which option is better or worse. However, when attempting to create a tribe (and then speak their language) it is more effective to connect over what feels more authentic to you first.

Once he'd created a tribe, Freud investigated. He lobbed the question of "What brings you here?" back to Darwin. Then, when Darwin didn't answer the question and asked a new one instead, Freud deflected to continue his own investigation. Darwin offered up a beige answer to Freud's inquiry, so Freud pressed him for more specifics and, finally, hit a nerve of sorts. "Lifesaving tech" has an emotional ring to it. Freud validated Darwin ("That's very noble of you") before investigating further, drawing out whether "lifesaving tech" was connected to Darwin's self-identity or value system, or if it was just a line he used in the world of investing.

Darwin, through sharing a personal story, revealed that "lifesaving tech" is uniquely important to him. Freud then validated with a genuine, "That's really cool." Validation can come from other words, nonverbals, or a combination of the two.

Note that Freud also validated an unspoken concern for Darwin. The venture capital world revolves around monetary returns. Sure, some great ideas rise to the top as obvious winners, but the venture-backed businesses that survive usually have solid financial plans too. Freud knew this and validated that fact, demonstrating his own awareness of the industry.

Finally, Freud related. He reiterated Darwin's viewpoint, phrasing his business idea in terms of Darwin's passion: "I'm building tech to help addicts recover." Lastly, Freud related directly, saying, "Saving lives is pretty important to me and my company too."

Every interaction is different, but this example displays some ways to uncover information about another person to connect and eventually cooperate. This conversation demonstrates how even two complete strangers, with seemingly nothing in common but a shared venue, can still form a connection. Freud could have sat next to any other venture capitalist, found some shared "language," and secured a pitch meeting—maybe a venture capitalist who was passionate about gaming, addiction, mental health, or partnering with insurance companies or health care providers.

Polite, honest conversation comes naturally to some people, but for others, it can be difficult to keep the conversation moving. Sometimes the other person isn't very talkative, or they start talking about

SPEAK THEIR LANGUAGE

an unfamiliar topic, and it's unclear how you might investigate, validate, or relate. In these circumstances, there are a few additional techniques that help us speak their language, even if the back-and-forth dialogue doesn't have much in common.

- **Mimicry:** When we're trying to connect with someone, we tend to subtly mimic their tone of voice, rate and rhythm of speech, speech melody, and syntax.[3] Even the simple act of speaking back the same words spoken by the other person can increase conversational benefits. Studies into mimicry show that it can yield positive results for the mimicker, like financial benefits, increased trust toward them, increased sales numbers, increased compliance toward requests, and increased perceived attractiveness. As an easy example, if the person you're speaking with talks slowly and quietly, you can slow your speech a little bit, add extra pauses, and lower your voice ever so slightly.
- **Active listening:** Active listening reflects empathy back at the person speaking, which has been shown to create more positive results during conversations.[4] We demonstrate active listening by mimicking, maintaining eye contact, asking open-ended questions, and offering unconditional positive regard for what the other person says. Studies focused on the effect of active listening on the listener's perceived impression show that when we use active listening skills, the people we listen to build a more positive opinion of us.
- **Open body language:** Our bodies communicate more than we think, especially when we're not actively adjusting them. Open body language, like upright posture, uncrossed arms, and uptilted chins, communicates openness—a willingness

to listen. Closed body language, like slumped shoulders, crossed arms or hands in pockets, and shifting gazes, makes us seem uninterested or even uncomfortable. We want to appear engaged in the conversation to increase trustworthiness.

Since every interaction is different, it isn't possible to lay out the perfect plan for speaking someone else's language. Instead, these basic strategies provide a selection from which we can pick and choose based on what feels right in the moment. People are naturally conversational, and as long as we make the effort to feel and foster comfort, we're one step closer to positively influencing the interaction.

Some of these strategies will fit perfectly into an influential interaction, while others may feel too clunky or forced. It's impossible to know with 100 percent certainty how your interaction partner will react to your conversational skills. That's why the best influencers and social engineers prepare themselves by learning the tools, preparing their techniques, and using that knowledge for quick adaptations.

Adapting to the Conversation

The art of influence requires a strong plan and a willingness to abandon that plan if the need arises. Make sure to conduct your research and planning beforehand, then allow for adaptations during the interaction. You must stay perceptive, picking up on subtle changes in conversational undercurrents. Then, when new information presents itself, use it to inform your approach and correct your course.

Sometimes, an attempt to make your interaction partner feel comfortable by sharing their language backfires. You might "strike a nerve" without intending to, which throws you off course and threatens to damage your budding relationship. If this happens to you, don't panic—there are ways to come back from a misstep. However, if you choose to push through the pain without correcting your approach, you're doomed to lose The Upper Hand.

A friend of mine once told me a story about a sales interaction that went sour in seconds, all because the saleswoman neglected to adapt after committing a conversational faux pas. My friend Aly was 19 and didn't know much about the ins and outs of the car-buying experience, so she brought her dad along to help her out. She found the car she wanted—a used 2018 Ford Fusion—and went to sign the paperwork. The saleswoman, who was friendly and helpful out on the floor, pivoted to make the hard sell.

"We've got several warranties here that can really make a difference in the life of the car," the woman said. "Do you want me to walk you through them?"

Aly looked to her father.

"We're not interested in any of the warranties," he said. "I've been working on Fords for years. I fully intend on fixing anything that goes wrong."

"I see," said the saleswoman, pursing her lips. "You know, these cars are much more complicated than they used to be. Take the AC unit, for example. The functionality is combined with the software in the main display. If the AC goes out, you'll have a bigger problem than a simple part switch."

"I'm sure we can manage," he said.

"I'm sure you could," she replied. Then she turned her attention to Aly.

"Aly," she started, "I know your dad thinks he's got this under control, but he's not going to be around forever, and you don't want your AC going out without a backup plan. And I'm sure he'd agree that he doesn't want his daughter driving around without AC in the dead heat of summer."

At that moment, Aly and her dad both steeled. They shared a look that said: this conversation is over. They let the saleswoman's words linger in the air, filling the space with their hostility. Aly's dad stared down the saleswoman like she was a bug he'd just scraped off his shoe.

"If you put down a single piece of paper that isn't the final sales agreement, we're walking out."

The saleswoman blanched, now clearly realizing she'd made a mistake.

"I understand you don't want a warranty, but at least let me—"

"No, he's right," Aly butted in. "Also, I would like to finish this deal with another associate. Who else do you have out on the floor today?"

With that, the pair left the saleswoman's office and finished the paperwork with someone else. By refusing to acknowledge her mistake, the saleswoman lost her commission, potential referrals, and returning customers. She chose to brute-force the sale instead of guiding it down her preferred path. When she had an opportunity to correct herself, she doubled down instead.

Her first mistake came when she avoided a crucial piece of information: Aly's dad works on cars. She didn't recognize their shared interest in the car industry, nor did she ask any follow-up questions. She wasn't interested in knowing whether his experience was professional or personal. Instead, she assumed that whatever experience he had, it fell short of what this car needed. What an insult!

Her second and third mistakes came in rapid succession: she invoked the eventual death of Aly's father. I don't think I'm making

SPEAK THEIR LANGUAGE

too strong of a statement when I say you should never use someone's impending death as a means for influence. Then, she immediately followed up her harrowing remark by implying that without this warranty, Aly's father would be dooming her to discomfort from beyond the grave! She thought that by directing these comments to Aly, she was softening the blow, but she only made the argument more offensive.

With a few small adjustments, the saleswoman could have made the interaction more pleasant for everyone. At any point in the conversation the woman could have investigated, validated, and related to better understand how to tailor her message about warranties and extra features to Aly and her dad.

Let's examine how this conversation could have benefited the saleswoman if she had tried speaking their language instead.

"We've got several warranties here that can really make a difference in the life of the car," the woman said. "Do you want me to walk you through them?"

Aly looked to her father, and he shook his head.

"We're not interested in any of the warranties," he said, "I've been working on Fords for years. I fully intend on fixing anything that goes wrong."

"Oh, that's great! My father was a car man, too, and he knew how to fix everything from a broken taillight to a blown gasket. Do you work in a shop, or do you work on cars for the fun of it?"

"I love cars," Aly's dad said, "and I had a similar experience with my dad. We used to spend more time working on our cars than we did driving them. There's almost nothing I can't tinker with from memory, and if there is, I can figure it out with a little research."

The saleswoman smiled and said, "Well, Aly, it seems like you've got a grade A mechanic here to help you out. Now, in just the last two years, these newer cars have integrated a lot more of their hardware with their software. Have you worked on a Ford since the overhaul?"

"I haven't," said Aly's dad, "but I'm an electrical engineer in my day job. I'm just as much of a software guy."

"That's excellent! Wow, an electrical engineer? You definitely seem like you've got this under control. Now, Aly, I do want to check in with you here—it sounds like your dad is the perfect mechanic. And that's a great solution for you as long as you live nearby. I know you said earlier that part of your reason for choosing this car is because you've put a lot of miles on your old one. Are you big into traveling?"

"I am," Aly said, nodding.

"I see," said the saleswoman, "and are you also planning on living locally for the next few years?"

"Well, my plan is actually to move further south eventually," she said. "The winters are a little too cold for my liking."

"Me too! Every winter I tell myself it's time to buy a condo in Miami," the saleswoman said with a laugh. "I just want to add, then, that if you're planning to move south or travel a long distance from home, you might be too far away for emergency car repairs if something goes wrong with the car. The warranty gives you and your dad peace of mind that if you have trouble anywhere in the US, the mechanic at any Ford dealer closest to your location can take a look and make some repairs for you, no problem. Even if they're just little fixes to hold you over until you make it back to Dad."

"That's a good point..." Aly said, looking at her dad. He shrugged. "Well, let's walk through some of those warranties, just in case."

This time, the saleswoman attempts to understand Aly and her dad's language before launching into a spiel. Instead, she investigated and validated Aly's dad's skills, and she withheld any judgments

SPEAK THEIR LANGUAGE

about his car-repair prowess. Then, she reinforced his skills by calling him Aly's personal mechanic. When he still refused the warranties, she adapted, pivoting her approach on a potential issue without insulting anyone. Again, he refused, but his refusal was a little more indirect, leaving her an opening to move on to Aly.

Here, the saleswoman related information Aly gave earlier. She validated and related to Aly's weather preferences, showing they shared the same opinions. Finally, she brought the sale back, and invoked a positive image, detailing how much easier her life could be if a grade A mechanic, like her father, was right around the corner at all times.

The saleswoman didn't agree with Aly or her dad about the choice to decline warranties, but that didn't stop her from continuing her influence strategy. In fact, most people who use influence are bound to run into resistance. The beauty of The Upper Hand strategy is that it's adaptable, and it takes into account that most people aren't immediately receptive to influence.

Like the Create a Tribe practice, the Speak Their Language practice is about connecting through honesty, authenticity, and openness. Sharing a language doesn't require you to agree with everything the other person says. Rather, it focuses on empathy and subtly guiding conversation. It's human nature to agree on some concepts and disagree on others. Part of what makes the human experience unique is that every person's worldview looks a little different. As long as your approach is based on finding the similarities between those worldviews to form a connection, you're on your way to earning The Upper Hand.

Chapter 7

PANTS YOURSELF

Sometimes, interactions take unexpected turns. We might make a faux pas, or fumble a simple handshake or hug. Sometimes people have bad days and take offense to a benign comment or request. They might blow a statement out of proportion, and if we're unsure of how to calm the other person down, we might find ourselves caught in an argument unrelated to our influence goals.

When interactions go astray, all is not lost, but course-correcting can be tricky. Every interaction requires at least two people, but you're only in control of what your side of the interaction can contribute. The other side might feel annoyed, distracted, uncomfortable, or they might feel some combination of these emotions. When you sense you're losing The Upper Hand, you can rein it back in with a showstopping move—you can Pants Yourself.

In one episode of *Parks and Recreation*, a popular American comedy series, one character literally pantses herself to take back The Upper Hand. Leslie Knope, deputy director of the Pawnee Parks and Recreation Department, agrees to host a charity telethon, but

THE UPPER HAND

instead of an easy daytime slot, she ends up hosting the night shift from 2 AM to 6 AM. Leslie tries her best to drum up viewers during her time slot, and she decides she needs something special to air.

Serendipitously, Leslie's friend and coworker, Mark, confesses to her that he plans to propose to his girlfriend, Ann. Ann is also Leslie's best friend. Leslie is thrilled for the two of them, then has an idea: she could use Mark's proposal as entertainment. Leslie convinces Mark to propose on camera during the telethon.

"On television, though?" Mark asks.

"Yes!" Leslie says, "We talked about it being something big, and I don't think we can get a hot air balloon this time of night."

"It would make a great story," Mark says during a confessional. "I trust Leslie."

So, Mark leaves the telethon to go home and grab his grandmother's ring. Leslie, thrilled about her brilliant idea to bring in some viewers and donations, announces a "really amazing thing" scheduled for the end of the telethon. She fills the time slots with more boring acts but keeps teasing viewers with an act they won't want to miss.

In the meantime, while Mark is still gone, Ann visits the telethon set to talk to Leslie.

"I think I need to break up with Mark," Ann says.

Leslie's eyes nearly pop out of her head.

"I've just been feeling for a while like something's missing," Ann continues, "and I kept thinking about the question you asked me before... about whether or not he's the one. And he's not."

"Mark really loves you," Leslie says, avoiding eye contact with Ann, "and I think he's ready to take this to the next step."

"He doesn't know what he's ready for," says Ann, "but I think I do."

PANTS YOURSELF

"Well," Leslie laughs, "I guess you're just going to have to marry him and figure it out!"

Ann looks at her sideways. "No...no."

"No! Why would you do that? Good for you, Ann," Leslie mumbles, and leaves her best friend confused and a little frustrated. Leslie rushes outside and calls Mark to tell him the proposal is off... but he doesn't answer.

The telethon timer ticks down to the final three minutes of Leslie's time slot, and she grows more anxious about Mark's whereabouts. Maybe it's a good thing Mark is late—then Leslie can avoid a disastrous on-air proposal and the embarrassment of her friend Ann. Leslie takes the microphone and goes onstage to break the news of a canceled surprise.

"I know we promised a special event coming up," she begins, but when Mark sneaks through the backstage crowd and waves the ring to Leslie, she's thrown off.

"Should I come up now?" Mark whispers from behind the camera.

Leslie shakes her head and whispers, "no," but Mark doesn't get the message. He comes up and joins her onstage, looking lovingly at Ann, who's manning one of the telethon's phone lines.

"No!" Leslie says again, thinking quickly. "What we're going to do is... we're going to pull our pants down! That's what we're going to do—everyone is going to pull their pants down for diabetes!"

Leslie unbuckles her pants, and the camera crew cuts to a "Technical Difficulties" screen. When the show returns, it's time for another local leader, Joan, to start her time slot.

"You just *love* flashing your ass, don't you?" Joan says with a smirk.

"When it's for a good cause, Joan," Leslie says quietly, rebuckling her pants.

Leslie's choice to pants herself is a little more literal than this Upper Hand practice suggests. But viewers of *Parks and Recreation* know Leslie's literal exposure is a physical representation of an emotional exposure. To viewers, Leslie held her feelings in for the entirety of the episode, but in finally being honest and vulnerable, she corrects the course of an interaction. In pantsing herself, Leslie halts the flow of Mark proposing, averting on-air embarrassment for both Mark and her friend Ann.

When I say to pants yourself, I'm not suggesting you literally pull your pants down—I'm referring to the practice of being vulnerable in front of the person or people you're influencing. Maintaining transparency, vulnerability, and authenticity provides the best foundation for genuine engagements with others, and proves you are worthy of others' trust. By being open with how you're feeling, you can let the other person off the hook for being resistant, stressed, or frustrated in an interaction. You can avoid losing The Upper Hand by drawing attention away from the tension in the interaction and turning it on yourself—you can pants yourself.

It's hard to be vulnerable with others, especially during high-stakes conversations. Vulnerability is risky because there's no guarantee you stand to gain anything by being transparent. It's this risk that drives others to clam up or avoid addressing the obvious rising frustration or tension in an interaction, particularly in a professional setting. People who grow frustrated in a business negotiation often keep their emotions to themselves, even when it's obvious they are upset.

When you pants yourself, you exert control over your interaction. Leslie, though she looked a bit ridiculous, did take back control of the situation. Ideally, we don't need to resort to literally pantsing ourselves to take back control. Pantsing yourself can be as simple as saying a few words.

Take back focus of the situation by expressing a bit of vulnerability. If an event-planning meeting begins to escalate, rather than calling out the rising tempers of two colleagues, call on your own feelings. You might say: "I apologize, everyone, but I'm getting frustrated, and I'd like a 10-minute break to regroup and reset. Is everyone okay with that?"

Had you called attention to your colleagues' emotional states instead of your own, it'd be the equivalent of pantsing *them*. Trying to pants others doesn't usually work. Again, many people are unwilling to be vulnerable, and pantsing them can come across as patronizing rather than empathetic, particularly in professional contexts.

Additionally, we often are unaware of the full context of others' emotional states. The two arguing colleagues in your meeting might be upset because of the topics you're all discussing, or it's possible they had a disagreement earlier in the day. Pantsing others often backfires.

When we pants ourselves, we give the other person an out. In a way, we take the fall without taking the blame, while we take back The Upper Hand by suggesting a course of action to resolve tension.

In other, more intense interactions, where you want to end the interaction—perhaps someone is so heated as to border on threatening—pantsing yourself allows you to exit the interaction with grace. There are some cases where an interaction is too far gone to maintain The Upper Hand. In these cases, it's better to end the interaction and try again another day than to keep pushing. To gracefully exit, you might say something like: "I don't feel like I'm being productive anymore today. Can we break and pick this up tomorrow morning?"

This isn't some magician's illusion meant to hide what's really going on from the other people in the room—it's simply a point of focus that you and others can use to break from, adjust, or end a high-pressure situation before it's ruined.

In the *Parks and Recreation* episode, Leslie follows up with Mark after pantsing herself to make sure he's okay. She catches him just as he's about to leave the television set. He's confused and frustrated.

"I'm sorry, Mark," Leslie says. "I think I was a little tired when I told you that you should do that. I don't think that's something Ann wants. Not on TV."

"So *that's* why you pulled your pants down," Mark says, smiling a little and relaxing his shoulders.

"Yeah," Leslie says. She blinks a few times, exhaustion taking over, then widens her eyes. "Wait, what did I do?"

When you pants yourself, it's like stopping a train hurtling for disaster. Instead of crashing and burning, you take the tension out of the room and let everyone off the hook gracefully. You offer an easy out for everyone involved and prevent emotions from tampering with your influence attempts. The interaction stops escalating and falls back under your control.

Why It Works: Mutual Self-Disclosure

Researcher and storyteller Brené Brown says, "Vulnerability is not about weakness; it's our greatest measure of courage." When we show vulnerability to others, we demonstrate honesty, transparency, and, most important for our purposes, trustworthiness. We make room for collaboration by clearing out any expectations of perfection or inauthenticity. We let other people know that although we're

PANTS YOURSELF

dressed up, spotlit, or leading the conversation, we're human beings first, and human beings don't always operate at full capacity. It takes courage to admit our imperfections, and it can be a relief when someone else does the same.

The power of vulnerability lies in trust. In layperson's terms, pantsing yourself shows humility and lets others know you don't take yourself too seriously. When you pants yourself, you make a proactive attempt to connect through emotions and experience. And often, this act of self-disclosure helps to relieve tension without forcing anyone else to be the butt of the joke (pun intended).

Pantsing yourself is an act of self-disclosure. Self-disclosure is a display of honesty and transparency, which promotes trust.[1] You're demonstrating to someone that you have nothing to hide. This practice can also shift the tide before it pushes you too far in the wrong direction.

In a way, pantsing yourself has a similar effect to taking off a restrictive pair of pants at the end of a long day. With one motion, you're free of a biting waistline, scratchy texture, and stuffy fabric. It's a relief to break out of the day's uniform and slide into a pair of sweats. It feels good to be free from the pressure.

Directly addressing the tension surrounding an interaction can also feel like a relief. A quick statement, like "Wow, I'm really nervous!" or "I'm a bit off today, so bear with me as we move forward," can make all the difference in an interaction's level of tension. These little moments of self-disclosure (vulnerability) show you are being honest and transparent.

If one person's mind is in a state of stress, tension, or fear, they may be more difficult to influence. When a person is caught in their own internal dialogue and sense of the world, it can be difficult for them to consider another person's lived experience. Pantsing yourself distracts from the other person's distractions, giving them time to feel more comfortable, confident, and competent.

The Pants Yourself practice is based in The Upper Hand's middle and pinky fingers—the human desires to connect, cooperate, and maintain a strong self-identity. By pantsing yourself during a stressful situation, you offer the interaction an opportunity to stop, reset, and begin again from a more cooperative place. You avoid insulting or embarrassing others, allowing them to maintain their self-identity and regain control over their emotional responses. Sometimes, a little pantsing is all it takes to break out of a high-pressure mindset.

A friend of mine named Kara spent a few months working in a surprisingly high-pressure environment: the Walt Disney World theme parks. The culture there was the epitome of "the customer is always right." One winter, Florida experienced an unusual cold snap. As soon as the golden sun dipped below the Cinderella castle, temperatures dropped from 60 degrees Fahrenheit to below freezing. The guests at the theme park were caught off guard by the cold, and every night, they flooded the gift shops to buy up all the blankets.

Except... it *is* Florida, and blankets aren't exactly high-demand products. In fact, there was only one blanket style in the entire park: a promotional product that customers received for spending $75 or more on other merchandise. Without that qualifying total, cashiers couldn't even ring the blanket up.

Customers surged like angry waves against the cash registers. In their defense, it was a high-pressure situation for them too—after spending thousands of dollars to make their kids feel real magic, they were now forced to either spend more money or let their kids freeze during the fireworks. It was probably that high stress that made them all refuse to acknowledge that maybe, just *maybe*, they should have checked the weather before heading out for the day. So instead, they screamed, stomped, and shook their freezing babies at the cashiers.

Kara, panicking as a small fight broke out over an Elsa beach towel, noticed something. Her register was teeming, but the one on the other side of the store seemed calmer. She could make out an actual line forming. The voices were quieter and slower. The cashier behind that counter, a young woman named Taryn, was *laughing*. What was going on over there?

"Hey, what's with Taryn's register?" Kara called to a coworker.

"Oh, people are giving her a break because she's still got the training badge."

The training badge! Of course! At Disney parks, new employees have a special training badge they wear for the first two weeks. It's a red ribbon with gold-threaded letters that say "Earning My Ears." These badges function for Disney employees like "Student Driver" stickers function on bumpers. They're meant to project the message: "Please spare me, I'm new!"

Kara ducked into the back and found a stray training badge. She slapped it below her name tag with a small smile. She knew some people still kept their training badges handy, but until now, she didn't know why.

Almost instantly, the crowd around Kara's register settled. Instead of screaming at her, customers gave her sympathetic smiles. They showed her patience when she couldn't immediately answer their questions. ("No, sorry, I don't know if the Sleeping Beauty dress-up costume is warmer than a T-shirt.") When she told them the blanket couldn't be rung up as a separate purchase, they sighed and left without arguing.

This is the real *magic*, Kara thought, straightening the training badge.

Disney's training badges allow new employees (and old ones who need a little break) to pants themselves to their customers. The badge self-discloses for the employee right away. When the customers see the badge, it reminds them the person behind the counter isn't some animatronic built to serve them Mickey-shaped pretzels—they're a human being, and they're still building up some confidence.

Not everyone can wear self-disclosure on their uniforms, but the lesson stands: pants yourself to earn some patience, empathy, and understanding from others. Whether you're at a theme park or in an office suite, sometimes the perfect way to deflate the tension is to remind others of your imperfections.

Imagine walking into a competitor's boardroom for a high-stakes meeting with the CEO. It's your team's responsibility to leave the meeting with a signed deal outlining a partnership between your businesses. Your career is riding on this one interaction, and if you leave empty-handed, you're bound to face some backlash. This CEO, Margaret Smith, has a reputation of being a no-nonsense-bordering-on-cutthroat businesswoman, and the idea of meeting with her sends you reeling.

When Margaret enters the boardroom, she's a few minutes late and still exudes a cool confidence. She's got a stack of prepared papers that sits taller than your whole briefcase. She's perfectly composed, and it only takes her a few minutes to settle in before signaling she's ready to start the meeting. *She doesn't look like a person,* you think to yourself, *she looks like a business robot.*

"Thank you for meeting with us today, and thank you for your patience. It's been one of those mornings," she says with a laugh. "Anyways, I know we're all aware of how important this meeting is for both of our companies, and I'm sure we're all a bit on edge. But

PANTS YOURSELF

let's not focus on the stakes. Let's focus on how we, as leaders in our industry, can come together to set new standards."

Her words invite the same kind of refreshment you'd feel if someone opened all the windows in the office. You know what "one of those mornings" means, even if the symptoms vary—traffic, cold coffee, mismatched socks, kids missing the bus—and you're reminded that Margaret *is* a person, just like you. No one rolled her out of the CEO-Bot Charging Closet just to take this meeting. She woke up this morning and faced one tiny blunder after another, just like you do sometimes.

At first, you had no way to know for sure if you were the only one feeling anxious. But when Margaret brought up her own anxiety along with everyone else's, the room became united under a common set of stakes. Finally, Margaret strengthened that unity by announcing a shared goal—a goal everyone was there to achieve.

In other words, Margaret pantsed herself, and everyone felt better.

Self-disclosure is crucial in developing and maintaining trust in any relationship.[2] It deepens interactions and allows people to understand each other on a deeper level. And self-disclosure often leads to *mutual self-disclosure*. When one person shares a vulnerability, people are more likely to share one of their own.

Mutual self-disclosure suggests that people share vulnerabilities with people they trust. Friends swap secrets because they trust each other not to share them beyond the group. Colleagues share gossip between office walls and trust they won't leave the building. At Disney's parks, the newbies' vulnerability isn't a secret, and they trust the customers to show kindness. At the very least, they trust their managers to support them if the badge doesn't protect them from the most impatient parkgoers. Mutual self-disclosure creates more connection and promotes successful, healthy, long-term relationships.

When you share a vulnerability, you extend trust to others, which gives them the opportunity to return it. This mutual display of trust is evidence you have The Upper Hand. If someone shares with you that they aren't at their best mentally, they must trust you're not going to use that information against them. They're more likely to trust you with their own vulnerabilities once you've shared yours with them.

Of course, there is always a risk that self-disclosure will not go as planned. Being vulnerable doesn't guarantee you'll be met with open arms. People might even feel more uncomfortable when you share a vulnerability. You might be rejected or dismissed. Worse, the information you disclose could be used against you. But the Pants Yourself practice is less about revealing deep dark secrets, and more about addressing the emotional elephants in the room.

Often, self-disclosure doesn't just help us wield The Upper Hand—it can make us feel better in an interaction.[3] Instead of struggling to stay composed when we are frustrated, anxious, or otherwise stressed, pantsing yourself can help you be more *you*. It takes cognitive effort to present a calm emotion while suppressing an uncomfortable feeling. Taking off our "masks" can be a cognitive relief.

The Pants Yourself practice is especially useful when the people around you aren't emotionally aware. If your coworker Steve's face is growing redder by the minute but he's too stubborn to take a deep breath, pantsing yourself might burst his rage bubble. Being vulnerable with him pumps the brakes on his own brain processes. In a professional context, being vulnerable can be jarring enough to interrupt the brain's automatic emotional thinking and allow for a moment of contemplative thought. Without interruption, Steve's anger will continue to build. Meeting Steve's anger with more intense emotions only fuels his emotional state. Instead, meet Steve's tension with the opposite: emotional release.

By showing vulnerability, you shine a light on the humanity hiding beneath your composure. It demonstrates that you are not the threat. Believe it or not, people prefer making deals with people more than they like working with chatbots or picture-perfect professionals.[4] They prefer sharing a common goal with someone who shows them empathy and compassion, not perfection or unrealistic behavior models. When highly competent people admit to a small pratfall, their colleagues tend to like them even more.[5] Seeing a leader pants themselves reminds us that, hey, we're all human here.

Don't Fake It

Like all good things, pantsing yourself works best in moderation. The first few times you use this practice, people will be relieved, understanding, and empathetic. But if you're consistently the first one to drop your emotional trousers the moment a situation gets a little tense, this technique will lose its potency. For this practice to remain effective, you must use it mindfully.

If you're not mindful about when and how you pants yourself, you run the risk of appearing manipulative, coercive, or deceitful. You must avoid presenting inauthentic vulnerabilities, sharing vulnerabilities in the wrong context, or pantsing yourself for the wrong reasons. Inauthentic motivations create inauthentic results.

There's a fine line between pantsing yourself as a solution and pantsing yourself as an excuse. Let's say your team has a massive presentation due at the end of the month, but one team member

(Steve again) hasn't finished their section. Instead of chastising Steve for slacking off, you inform the higher-ups that you'd like more time to prepare yourself. This is all new material, you explain, and the more time you have to prep, the more likely you are to succeed. They understand and give you an extra week. Great!

Meanwhile, you approach Steve and ask him how you can help him finish his section. He responds with, "This content is confusing, I don't have enough time to finish, and I'm just going to do it wrong anyway. Could you just do it for me?" He looks up at you with sad, puppy dog eyes, and you catch yourself before you say yes.

Steve has pantsed himself here, but once you move past the initial emotional response, you realize his adaptive tactic. He's using self-deprecation to get out of doing the work. He's giving an excuse without a solution. He shows a vulnerability—a lack of confidence and time. He *wants* you to feel sorry for him and take the work off his plate.

When people expose vulnerabilities to gain sympathy instead of empathy, it makes others uncomfortable. In this example, since you're an empathetic person, Steve's pantsing prompts you to want to comfort him, disagree with his self-deprecation, or present a solution for him. Realistically, none of these options solve the problem at hand. You don't have a real solution, and you're probably feeling *more* stressed instead of relieved.

Steve's tactic provides a short-term solution—you're out of time here, so you take on his share of the work. However, next time you have a presentation like this, you're less likely to invite Steve to contribute. Instead of fostering collaboration, Steve showed you he can't be trusted to finish the job. He took advantage of your empathy. He may think his pantsing gave him The Upper Hand in the short term... but when he sees the pink slip on his desk a few months later, he knows he made a mistake.

Pantsing yourself requires genuine vulnerability to be effective. Operating from an inauthentic place to make excuses, ignore responsibilities, or distract from mistakes doesn't result in true influence—it makes others mistrustful and uncomfortable. Only by being transparent, authentic, and vulnerable can you prove yourself trustworthy and create a foundation for genuine interactions.

It's crucial to use the Pants Yourself technique mindfully and ethically. It's not about faking vulnerability or using it as a manipulative tactic. Instead, it's about sharing your true emotions and concerns to bring people back together, reinforcing your efforts toward a common goal and a shared sense of understanding.

How to Pants Yourself

Why is this technique called "Pants Yourself"? It's because it's a way to openly, honestly, and ethically expose yourself to the people around you. Share your emotions. Share your concerns. Address the "but" in the room... as long as you say it's *your* "but" (yes, this pun again). Presenting your shortcomings without passing judgment on them helps reduce intimidation, increase connection, and disrupt stress responses.

If you recognize someone else is suffering during an interaction—whether they're squirming under pressure, struggling to make a decision, or looking for an excuse to leave—pantsing yourself avoids derailing your strategy. Some people might decide to address the issue directly by pointing it out. "Steve, I sense you're upset. Would you rather talk about this later?" Sure, this method shows emotional awareness, but it also might embarrass Steve. It's an accusatory statement. You might seem like the one with The Upper Hand, but in reality, you've actually made Steve less receptive to your influence.

Instead, you can set Steve free from his stressed emotional state, letting him out of the interaction without blame. Pants yourself by saying, "I'm sorry, I want to solve this problem together, but I'm losing my composure a bit. Can we come back to this later?" You've still addressed the issue directly this way. But by taking on the blame, you've also taken control of the interaction.

When you use the Pants Yourself practice, it's important to remain composed. Keep a level tone and calm body language, and make a simple statement about your feelings. When you express your emotions, make sure your statement is free from blame. For example, "I feel ignored" isn't an emotion; it's an interpretation of what someone else is doing. Instead, focus the statement on yourself: "I'm struggling to express my ideas in a way that's easy to comprehend, and I'm getting frustrated."

Once you have stated the emotional component, suggest a time to reconvene. The new time will depend on the situation. Sometimes five-minute breaks are easy to fit in. Other times, it might be a week before you can meet with the other person again.

When the situation is diffused, you can set a new strategy to gain The Upper Hand. If you choose to regroup after a short break, take a few minutes to read the room when you reconvene. If everyone's feeling calmer, great! You can carry on with the interaction. However, if the tension is still in the room with you, it might be best to start over on a new day. Offer a follow-up meeting or reconnect with a text or email the next day. This approach gives everyone a chance to disconnect, reflect, and come back with fresh energy.

PANTS YOURSELF

The Pants Yourself practice is valuable when seeking The Upper Hand because it acknowledges that some interactions veer off course. Influence isn't always smooth. People make mistakes, grow frustrated, get distracted. This practice gives agency back to influencers when negotiations don't go perfectly. And in some cases, it can right the course of the interaction immediately.

Not even master influencers operate without error all the time. Pantsing yourself destigmatizes the fumbles, blunders, and pratfalls we all experience in our everyday lives. It brings some levity to any interaction and reminds all involved of our humanity. After all, the most ethical influence cannot function without the constant reminder that we're all human, and we're all working toward the same wholesome goals.

There's a sense of freedom you gain when you embrace the power of pantsing yourself. It feels good to acknowledge unspoken tension. It's nice to know others feel the same undercurrents of emotions in any given interaction. By bringing attention to it, you make it easier to solve.

By practicing empathy, understanding, and vulnerability by pantsing ourselves, we can create more harmonious and respectful relationships in our daily interactions. The next time you find yourself stuck in a stressful, frustrating, or overwhelming situation, fear not! You can always find a safe way out by pantsing yourself.

Chapter 8

SHELVE IT

The practice in the previous chapter, Pants Yourself, covers how to share information with others to make your interactions more successful. The practice you're about to learn, Shelve It, covers the opposite. Shelve It is a practice in figuring out when to *hold back* information to earn and keep The Upper Hand.

Imagine you're about to sit down at your desk to work. You reach for your computer mouse, but it's blocked by errant books, pens, and papers. While each of these items are important tools you use throughout your day, right now, they're distractions. When your main goal is to check your email, anything in your way is simple clutter.

Later in the day, when you need a pen and paper, your mouse might get in your way too. Your background music is invaluable during concentrated work sessions, but it's a hindrance during meetings. Your team's messaging channel is useful when you have questions for your coworkers, but when its incessant *ding* notifications pull you out of your work, it creates an obstacle to work.

Each of these items is important to your daily work, but they're all important at different times, for different reasons, and in different contexts. How do you clear enough space to work throughout the day while still keeping your tools within reach? You bring the ones you need to the center of your work, and you put the rest away for when you need them. In other words, you shelve them.

When you use the Shelve It practice, you take inventory of the tools on your inner shelf and strategically decide what to use, what to ignore, and what to push away to avoid temptation. As you work toward gaining influence, there are bound to be some parts of yourself better left to the side, so you can focus on successful outcomes. Any tools you sometimes use that may cause rifts in an influence interaction—personal biases, beliefs, and emotional impulses—stay on the shelf.

Since The Upper Hand has you operating from a place of open communication, some of your interactions are bound to take surprising twists and turns. Some conversations may divert into topics that make you uncomfortable, frustrated, or even upset. They may infringe on your personal beliefs, or they may inspire a gut reaction to argue against them. However, if you want to maintain The Upper Hand, you can't be distracted by these small diversions from your influence strategy. Instead, you can acknowledge them, dismiss them, and redirect the conversation back to your ultimate goal.

During influential interactions, reacting strongly to information, especially in a negative way, is risky. It's one matter to react with enthusiasm ("You grew up near Grayshott? No way, so did I!"), because the energy spike *could* throw someone off, but they're more likely to match your energy than dismiss it when it comes from a commonality. However, it's another matter when your reaction is negative ("You like *pop music?* I'd never be caught dead listening to

SHELVE IT

Lady Gaga."), because it makes the person you're speaking with feel resistance. Your response might be authentic, but your authenticity could cause them to bristle, which will throw off your strategy.

You can avoid causing unnecessary resistance by employing the Shelve It practice. If you're trying to influence Valerie, the CEO, and she mentions that she knows the earth is flat, you might feel it's your responsibility to tell her she's wrong. However, she's more likely to dislike your response (and dislike you) than she is to hear you out. Instead, shelve it. Maintain a respectful demeanor by nodding politely. Acknowledge her (through gritted teeth, perhaps) with a neutral phrase like, "That's an interesting perspective. It reminds me of . . ." then slowly steer the conversation back to what you have in common—a goal that has nothing to do with the curvature of the earth.

Now, as you'll see later in the chapter, not every interaction is well suited for the Shelve It practice. It's worth keeping in mind that your opinions, beliefs, and emotions may not help you during influence attempts. Keep the three C's in mind: comfort, competence, and confidence. You must ensure your interactions take place in a comfortable environment, not a space for arguments. You want to project confidence, not arrogance. And, finally, you want everyone involved to feel competent enough to contribute to the interaction, which is hard to do when you're trapped in a heated debate.

By shelving your emotional reactions, your personal opinions, and any other factors unnecessary for influence, you keep them in mind without drawing attention to them. Later, when the interaction is finished and your influence is successful, those items are still on the shelf waiting for you. This practice isn't about removing parts of yourself or hiding them from view—it's about temporarily setting aside the things that may impact your influence strategy.

Dusting the Shelf: Emotional Intelligence

The Shelve It practice is, at its core, emotional discipline. Humans are emotional beings, and our emotions sometimes trigger us to act without critical thought. But once we take action, we can't take it back. When we shelve a strong emotional reaction, we limit the potential damage our emotional responses can cause on our interactions.

There's an old story by an unknown author that teaches the importance of emotional discipline. It goes by many names, but I call it "The Boy with the Temper."[1] It goes like this:

There once was a little boy who had a very bad temper. His father handed him a bag of nails and said that every time the boy lost his temper, he had to hammer a nail into the wooden fence.

On the first day, the boy hammered 37 nails into the fence.

Gradually, the boy began to control his temper, and the number of nails he hammered into the fence slowly decreased. He discovered it was easier to control his temper than to hammer those nails into the fence.

Finally, the day came when the boy didn't lose his temper at all. He told his father the news, and the father suggested that the boy should now pull out a nail every day he kept his temper under control. The days passed and the young boy was finally able to tell his father that all the nails were gone. The father took his son by the hand and led him to the fence.

"You have done well, my son, but look at the holes in the fence. The fence will never be the same. When you say things in anger, they leave a scar just like this one. It won't matter how many times you say 'I'm sorry.' The wound is still there."

SHELVE IT

It's likely that many of us have driven nails through conversations without thinking about the scars they leave behind. When it comes to influence, it's crucial we leave the nails on the shelf for safekeeping instead of hammering them into others. Even if we win an argument, make valid points, or succeed at changing minds, we do so at the expense of keeping The Upper Hand.

If you struggle to stop yourself from reaching for the nails in a conversation, you might benefit from stronger emotional discipline. Emotional discipline comes from emotional intelligence, which is your level of awareness, control, and expression of your emotions. This may seem like a simple skillset, but many people find it deceptively difficult.

Emotional intelligence can be broken down into three main skills: self-awareness, self-control, and self-regulation. People with high emotional intelligence are masters of their own emotions. They can recognize an emotional spike, identify the cause, resist the urge to act on it, and bring themselves back to baseline. The stronger their emotional intelligence, the more control they have over their interactions with others.

The first skill, self-awareness, refers to how well you recognize your own emotions. A person with strong self-awareness can answer the following questions without hesitation: What makes you angry? What calms you down? What makes you sad? What excites you? What are you most afraid of? Once you're aware of what causes you to feel strong emotions, you can adjust your approach to different environments.

Self-control refers to how well you respond to emotional spikes. Say you're the world's biggest fan of Taylor Swift, and Bryce from the office is trashing her newest album. Do you engage and argue with him? Do you ignore him? Do you offer your opinion but accept her music isn't for everyone? You might be furious at Bryce's obtuse, uncultured taste, but how you choose to express that emotion depends on how well you control it. No matter how amazing Taylor's album is, it's probably not worth you exploding with rage and losing your job.

Finally, self-regulation refers to how efficiently you reduce a spike in emotions. Bringing yourself back down from a fit of rage, a moment of panic, or a burst of uncontrollable laughter is no small task. Emotional responses affect the entire body. Your heart rate and blood pressure rise. Your muscles tense. Your breathing shifts. Whether they cause you to buzz with energy or faint from overwhelm, your emotional responses are distracting. The better your self-regulation, the faster you can calm your response and resume interactions with others.

If emotional responses are natural, why must we spend so much time and energy fighting them? If you want to scream at your coworker for trash-talking about your interests, doesn't that desire come from somewhere natural inside of you? The easy answer is, yes, your emotional responses *are* natural, but like plenty of evolutionary traits they haven't caught up with modern social norms.

Our emotional responses are driven by our fight-or-flight response, which is helpful in some situations and outdated in others. If you run into a bear in the woods, your fear would motivate you to break into a mad dash. Or, if your brain thinks you could take the bear, you might feel a sense of rage that causes you to sock the bear right in the nose. In today's modern world, we're much more likely to run into social danger than physical danger, but our psychological responses have a hard time telling the difference.

This is why it sometimes feels so good to retaliate in a social situation. When we secure the last word, deliver a witty comeback, or "win" an argument, our brains process the win as equal to a swift punch to a bear snout.[2] It makes us feel like we're taking back control from whatever triggered the spike in our emotions—fear, embarrassment, anger, etc.—and therefore handling a threat.

While it might feel good temporarily to prove another person wrong, it can come at the cost of your relationship. Interactions between the two of you will become tense if you start a feud in the wrong place at the wrong time. If your interaction partner is equally poor at self-control, the argument might escalate and threaten your safety. Even if you're arguing in favor of a topic that resonates with who you are at your core, it's best to take how you feel and shelve it—at least until you've secured The Upper Hand.

In extreme situations, your emotional reactions can put you in real danger. Take, for example, cases of road rage—bursts of anger, aggression, or even violence from motorists. When someone cuts you off in traffic or swerves without warning, you're likely to swell with anger. That anger comes from your fear for your own safety. If you act on emotional impulse, you might throw up a middle finger, honk your horn in anger, or toss a string of curse words out the window as the offender passes. If they see or hear you, it's likely they'll grow angry too. And when two angry people confront each other on the road, the results are often far more dangerous than they are on foot.

Most drivers experience some form of road rage. In fact, the average driver experiences about 27 instances of road rage in their life.[3] Feeling road rage is one thing, but acting on it is a totally different experience. The people who lash out at other drivers as a result of road rage put themselves, and others, in danger.

Why are people so unwilling to shelve their road rage?

Psychologists believe it's because they're not actually thinking about the other people inside the cars around them:

"The heavy metal of a car is a safe haven," remarked Ava Cadell, PhD, during an interview concerning road rage accidents. "Road ragers don't think about the consequences or even about other people on the road as real people with real families."

When you don't consider the person behind the other wheel, you don't consider how dangerous they can be. They might be prone to violence. They might have a gun, and they might be willing to use it. In fact, in the United States alone, at least 413 people were injured or killed by road rage incidents involving a gun in 2022. These incidents translate to an average of one person shot, injured, and/or killed every 16 hours.

Although you might feel justified cursing at a truck while it passes you illegally on the shoulder, it's best to shelve your anger. Cars are dangerous enough on their own—it's in drivers' best interest to minimize risk when on the road. You don't want to risk your own safety for the sake of being right about traffic laws. You never know how far the other driver will go to feel superior over you.

In an influential interaction, responding to surprise deviations like a rage-ridden driver will only cause you to fail. If you decide to chastise your interaction partner for making the wrong decision, however small it may be, you'll lose them altogether. You'll stop making them feel comfortable and trigger their stress response instead. Then, they'll either dive into a rage-fueled argument with you, or they'll flee the scene as fast as possible. Either way, they'll lose trust in your ability to collaborate and, worst of all, the next time they're out and about, they'll avoid coming across your path ever again.

Shelve It is hard to learn because it requires emotional discipline, but it's a skill anyone can learn. However, before going through some pointers on how to practice, it might help to understand *why* this technique works. I hope you don't find the commonalities with real-world shelves too surprising.

Why It Works: Shelve It

Shelves help us declutter. At home, shelves provide storage for all kinds of useful items—kitchen cabinets for dishes and utensils, garden shelves for trowels and pots, and bookshelves for, well, books. Putting things away on their assigned shelf creates the space you need to be productive. You can't use kitchen counters if they're cluttered with every dish you own. You can't garden if the plot is full of spare pots. You can't work at your desk if it's covered in your favorite books. You need space to work, and shelves help provide it.

When you choose to shelve difficult emotions, objections, and distractions during an interaction, what exactly are you creating space for? The answer is connection. Emotions, objections, and distractions are points of possible contention. When you clear out your differences, you leave more room for commonalities.

With points of contention out of the way, people feel more comfortable and safer in interactions. This is necessary if they are to share information—especially private information. People are also more likely to feel comfortable entering into a collaboration when there are no obstacles in their way. When emotions, objections, and distractions are placed on the shelf, what's left is a safe, comfortable space for establishing connections and forming trust.

If you know the person you must interact with is fundamentally different from you, then it's in your best interest to shelve it. You may sit on opposite sides of the political aisle. You may have opposing views, beliefs, or moral standards. However, in an influence interaction, what matters is what you have in common. Any differences will only get in the way.

Instead of focusing on your thoughts and feelings, shelve them and focus instead on the other person's wants, needs, and goals. This doesn't neglect or remove your own motivations—they're on the shelf, not in the garbage—but it does allow you to tailor your influence strategy more effectively to the person in front of you.

The Shelve It practice is most valuable in the exact situations where it's the hardest to use. It's heavily based on The Upper Hand's pinky finger: the self-identity preservation instinct. However, this principle is also what makes Shelve It so tempting to ignore. I'm talking about moments in interactions when someone, either accidentally or on purpose, makes a remark about something you consider near and dear to who you are. This insult cascades through all the Upper Hand digits—it threatens your identity, spikes your heart rate from anger, and makes your desire to cooperate fizzle out. Depending on the severity of the insult, it might even make you feel like your safety is at risk. I've had people comment on my size as a compliment before, but saying, "You're so small, I could throw you across the room!" doesn't exactly foster feelings of safety.

In these moments, shelving your rebuttal can feel more like you're betraying yourself than saving your chances of success. But choosing to act on your emotional response could cost you that elusive "yes," so you must proceed with caution. A small verbal victory feels good in the moment, but that feeling fades if your actions also tank the deal.

Most of us have experienced situations like these, although the severity of them varies. A friend of mine once went to a job interview in a business casual suit. Since the interviewer couldn't see my

SHELVE IT

friend's full tattoo sleeve, he didn't realize his faux pas when he mentioned the last interviewee came in with "those ridiculous doodles" all over their arms.

"It's not technically against policy," the interviewer said, "but it's obviously unprofessional."

My friend was tempted to rip off her suit jacket just to see the look on the interviewer's face when he realized his mistake. She also considered offering up a different opinion, letting him know that for some people, tattoos are a form of self-expression that doesn't indicate their level of professionalism. Instead, she nodded politely and took a long sip from a glass of water. The interviewer filled in the silence by starting the official interview.

Another friend of mine was waiting for a pitch meeting to begin when one man—the other team's lead—made a cutting remark about an Ivy League university. My friend, having graduated from the university mentioned, had to shelve a knee-jerk response to defend his alma mater. He knew his defense would only set him apart from these people, and he needed to focus on what they had in common if he wanted to sell them on his pitch.

A third friend had a date rescheduled at the last minute for a time when her kids would be home. She needed a babysitter on short notice, so she called up her brother. He agreed, but only on the condition that she go see *Fast X* with him in theaters that weekend. Instead of reminding her brother that she *hated* action movies, or that she hadn't seen the previous movies in the franchise, she shelved her objections and agreed. After all, she was getting what she wanted, and a movie with her brother was a small price to pay.

The Shelve It practice helps you get out of your own way when it comes to influence. It gives you the space you need to connect. When the moment comes when you know a clever comeback isn't the solution, but the opportunity is *just so tempting*, having the emotional discipline to make the right choice can be a huge asset. Learning to have emotional discipline, though, is a process. So, let's explore how to train this skill.

How to Shelve It

Since the Shelve It practice is all about emotional discipline, it requires two base skills: mindfulness and empathy. In practice, knowing how to shelve it means knowing how to control your internal and external reactions to situational surprises. Mindfulness and empathy will help you manage your emotional reactivity. So, to learn how to shelve it, we'll start by exploring a way to practice mindfulness and empathy, then we'll dive into how to manage emotional reactivity in the moment.

Not many people recognize the importance of mindfulness and empathy in business, but those who do see unprecedented success. Their knowledge, understanding, and control over their own minds equip them to relate to the minds of others. To train these skills, there is one practice that engages them both: mindful meditation.

Mitch Presnick, the franchise founder for Super 8 in China from chapter 1, is a big proponent of mindful meditation. He's been meditating for over three decades, and he credits this practice with his strong sense of empowerment, self-control, and empathy. In our discussion about his business success, he said, "There are two kinds of people: people who have mastered their minds, and people who have been mastered by their minds."

He's correct in this attribution. Studies have shown meditation is beneficial to sustained attention, response inhibition, and cognitive functions like critical thinking and decision-making strategies.[4] By mastering his own mind, Mitch has also mastered his strategy for gaining The Upper Hand.

When Mitch sets out to gain The Upper Hand in his interactions, he starts with empathy. He strategizes from the perspective of the person he wants to influence, not from inside his own head. "I don't focus on what it would take for me to succeed first," he said. "I want to figure out what success looks like for them, and then see how I could fit into that image."

When Mitch approached the Super 8 board, he shelved any tactics that distracted from his goal. He could have designed a strategy around how American franchises saw great success, and used data from his home country to demonstrate the potential in China. Businesspeople have tried and failed to prove potential by comparing one country to the other. However, Mitch knew better. He recognized this approach wouldn't draw attention to the similarities between America and China—it would only serve to show the differences. Instead, he shelved his notions about American success and collected data on the Chinese market as it stood then.

By setting aside the tempting comparisons between these two vastly different countries, Mitch made room for research that addressed what this panel *actually* considered important: the future of the hotel industry in China. He connected with their shared interest in forging a path to a new kind of business model in China. This successful connection helped the panel trust him. Ultimately, the panel decided their decision to work with him would be a safe, comfortable choice. And Mitch's eventual business wins proved the panel correct.

There's bound to be some resistance whenever you practice influence, and if the resistance comes unexpectedly, it can be discouraging or even overwhelming. The more resistance you face, the harder it is to shelve your emotions of frustration or disheartenment. If you're not prepared for this possibility, you may end up snagged by your own emotional reactivity and plunged into a downward spiral of negative emotions. Meditation and mindfulness strengthen your ability to respond to resistance without any emotions, objections, or distractions in the way.

Mindfulness, often built up through meditation, has been shown to decrease emotional reactivity. In one study, people were assigned a number of tasks and asked to complete them while presented with emotionally disturbing images.[5] Those who practiced mindful meditation could more easily disengage from the images and refocus on each task. Those who didn't meditate were regularly distracted. Those who meditated had an easier time putting their negative emotions on the shelf, leaving cognitive space for critical thinking and decision-making.

Holding back emotional reactivity is the core of the Shelve It practice. Holding back frustration, confusion, annoyance, offense, and other common emotional responses during tricky influence situations is hard. But by setting aside your reactions, you also set aside any friction in your interaction. This technique mitigates the risk of insulting, discomforting, or creating resistance in the person you're trying to influence.

Recognizing the importance of the Shelve It practice, especially in business-based influence interactions, can lead to unparalleled success at securing The Upper Hand. Mastering your own thoughts and emotions can enhance your ability to understand and connect with others. This gives you the strongest chance for achieving your ultimate goal—successful, ethical influence.

When it comes to using the Shelve It practice *in the moment*, there are two components to be aware of: your inner and outer response. Emotional reactivity manifests both in your head and through your behavior, and it's not enough to only master one. If you can't control your inner reactivity, then your emotions, objections, and distractions will show on your face. And if you can't control your outer reactivity, then your thoughts will likely be derailed too. So, let's see how we can apply mindfulness and empathy to managing our inner and outer reactivity.

On the Inside

The first step you'll want to take when an emotional reaction takes you by surprise is to acknowledge it. Yes, that comment about your weight was uncalled for. Of course, a remark that undermines your effort is frustrating. It's normal to feel bristled when someone makes an incorrect assumption about you. Just because you don't plan to address your emotional response in the moment doesn't mean it's not worth addressing at all—your response is valid.

If you don't acknowledge your own distress, it's bound to buzz around in your mind like a persistent fly, distracting you from the task at hand. Make a mental note to revisit the issue once your interaction is over. That way, your stress response recognizes you're taking action, even if the action is postponing action. This allows you to level out your internal cortisol levels, which will help you refocus on the next step of your interaction.

You can recognize your emotional experience once the interaction is over, in the right time and place. Taking this step avoids a negative impact on your emotional regulation process. If you restrain an emotional response without addressing it later, you risk damaging your sense of self-trust. It's okay to shelve your emotions in the moment, but if you ignore them forever, your shelf will end up cluttered and disorganized. It'll become more difficult to take the useful items down when they're blocked by pent-up emotions.

Once you have a free moment outside of the interaction, conduct a self-assessment—a shelf-tidying—to realign with your self-trust. As an example, let's imagine an interaction where your friend announced their engagement to a man you can't stand. You've told her in the past how you feel about him, and sometimes she seems like she sees your points, but she always ends up back on his arm. When you heard the news, you shelved your disappointment and congratulated her in the moment, but now you're not sure you made the right choice.

You can ask some self-assessing questions to better understand the situation. Will future interactions with your friend be more difficult now that you've shelved your emotions? Are you planning to address what's on your shelf at a later, more appropriate date? Does your emotional response still feel as strong now that you're out of that interaction, or did the context cause a stronger reaction than expected?

In this scenario, hiding your feelings about your friend's new fiancé *could* affect future interactions. So, you realize you *do* need to address your feelings, but you're confident that her announcement wouldn't have been the right moment to do so. Now that you've had some time to sit with the idea, you know your emotional response stems from a true concern for your friend's future happiness and not from a petty dislike of her fiancé. Your emotional response in the moment was valid, you decide, and so was your decision to shelve it.

Now that you've processed your perspective and your emotional response, you can decide how to move forward. You set a time to meet with your friend and address your worries for her. However, instead of reacting impulsively with protests or complaints, you can form an empathetic inquiry that either helps you feel confident in your friend's choice or helps her recognize some issues to address with her fiancé. Either way, the outcome is your friend's happiness— but if you'd reacted on emotional instinct, the outcome may have been the end of your friendship.

On the Outside

The best reaction to a surprising digression is no reaction. The more you can do to appear unfazed, focused, and nonchalant, the more you'll aid your own influence. However, maintaining a solid poker face requires a strong grasp on emotional regulation skills.

If you can limit any nonverbal cues that broadcast sudden changes in temperament, you're more likely to keep The Upper Hand. Resist the urge to self-soothe with gestures like rubbing your neck, face, or arms. Try not to bounce your legs, shuffle your feet, or adjust your position. Redirect your attention from your own emotions to the emotions of the person you're interacting with—this will help you mirror their nonverbal cues instead of tipping anyone off with your own.

Take the time you need to form a rational, strategic response to what triggered you to shelve it. You can help along your emotional regulation process with a series of deep breaths. As you bring yourself back down to a calm, balanced demeanor, your pause can be powerful. The other people in the room don't need to know you're collecting yourself—they may think you're wielding the pause like a banner of confidence.

While you work to regain emotional balance, you can weigh your options for moving forward. What is the risk of addressing your concern versus the reward of shelving it? How can this information, should you choose to shelve it, be useful in further interactions? If you turn and run from your friend after her engagement announcement, you risk making her angry with you. However, if you choose to address your concerns later, you can renew past conversations about her problematic fiancé with the added weight of a wedding—and a marriage—for her to consider.

It may feel uncomfortable to let silence linger between you and your interaction partner, but sometimes silence can work in your favor. If the statement that set you off was rude, offensive, or incorrect, letting it hang in the air like a noxious cloud may cause the person who said it to self-correct. Silence is also useful when you're hoping to elicit information from others—people grow uncomfortable in long silences, and they often fill it with valuable information.

Shelving your emotions is a valuable practice for keeping an interaction on track. The Upper Hand requires some strategy, but it's also crucial to develop emotional intelligence skills so you can adapt in real time to surprises. However, as is true with all Upper Hand principles, the Shelve It practice isn't a one-size-fits-all solution. There are some situations in which shelving your emotions is actually the *wrong* move. If your goal is an ethical, meaningful collaboration with another person, there may come a time when letting your response flow freely is the only way to make it happen.

When to Ignore the Shelf

How often do people pronounce your name incorrectly? It seems like no matter how simple any given person's name appears, there's always someone who pronounces it wrong. A friend of mine, Corrine,

SHELVE IT

pronounces her name "Curr-inn." She's gotten all kinds of funny and embarrassing attempts to pronounce it—"Core-een," "Core-eye-n," and some that aren't even close, like Karen, Korean, or Corn. Sometimes she finds it annoying, but other times, she just laughs it off.

Since Corrine's name is mispronounced more often than not, she's not quick to correct people on it. She knows from experience that people are usually embarrassed after they're corrected, and she doesn't like to make people feel that way. Instead, she shelves her corrections to make them feel more comfortable interacting with her. This practice isn't a big deal when she neglects to correct a barista, a checkout clerk, or a receptionist, but sometimes she avoids correcting people she's bound to run into again... which creates an issue.

A few years back, Corrine took an interview for a new job. She didn't correct the interviewer when he called her "Core-een," because she didn't want to start the meeting by correcting someone. She nailed the interview, and when her second interview started, again she refused to correct him when he introduced her to a panel. When the CEO called Corrine to her office for an introduction, she didn't correct their pronunciation either. It wasn't until her first official day at work that she realized how big her mistake had grown.

Every time Corrine met someone new in the office, she had to choose: *do I pronounce my name correctly, or do I use the pronunciation other people are using?* If she said her name correctly, she increased the odds of the interviewer, panel, and CEO finding out she never corrected them throughout her hiring process. If she pronounced it incorrectly, she'd end up labeled with a name nowhere near her own. Would she even respond if someone called out, "Hey 'Core-een,' come here!"? She doubted it.

For weeks, Corrine couldn't decide what to do... until someone made the choice for her. It was a man named Peter, who came from an outside organization and was in the middle of a roll call.

"Corrine?" he called out, correctly pronouncing her name.

"It's actually Core-een," said the CEO, winking at her.

"Is it?" Peter asked. "That's my daughter's name too."

Both looked at Corrine with confusion. Her face flushed. She offered a small, apologetic smile to her CEO.

"Oh my god!" the CEO exclaimed, "you've been here a month! You never told me I was pronouncing your name wrong!"

Corrine's initial choice to shelve it came from the desire to save others from embarrassment, but she ended up creating *more* embarrassment later. She embarrassed herself by refusing to address a problem, and she embarrassed the people she worked with by letting them continue to call her by the wrong name. Plus, her CEO was both confused and a little frustrated by Corrine's failure to fix something as important as the way people at work identified her.

While it's helpful to shelve it for small incongruencies between interaction partners, some concessions actually decrease the possibility of building a relationship. If the other person reveals they're against one of your core beliefs, you're not likely to build trust with them. If they take an action that violates your moral code, you may feel more comfortable ending the interaction than shelving your reaction. We can still leave these situations respectfully, but we must leave them, or we risk losing The Upper Hand.

The Shelve It practice helps you step out of your own way. However, humans are biologically, socially, and psychologically designed to stand in our own ways when we're in danger. We must keep this in mind when we choose to shelve it—we're clearing space

SHELVE IT

for cooperation, not hiding valuable responses from ourselves and others. We can't openly and ethically collaborate with others if our shelves are cluttered with secret feelings and beliefs. Instead, we can have meaningful interactions that result in successful influence by picking and choosing what goes on the shelf.

Chapter 9

HOLD, DON'T SQUEEZE

The handshake is a powerful nonverbal tool. It's a gesture that transcends most cultures, taking precedence over bows, pecks on the cheek, and hugs between two people from different countries meeting. By reaching out for a handshake, humans signal trust and a willingness to cooperate. Through physical contact, we trigger a release of oxytocin, the bonding hormone. A handshake may seem like a simple gesture, but it's a telling one too.

There is a subtle art to mastering the perfect handshake. For one, you must know your audience to know what kind of pressure to apply when shaking a stranger's hand. Different cultures have different handshaking etiquette. Some cultures prefer strong, short handshakes, while others make introductions with short, gentle grasps. Sometimes, gender plays a role in who initiates the handshake, or who avoids them altogether.[1] Once you have a foundational understanding of what others need from your introduction, you can master the best approach for influencing them.

In America, there is a balance struck in a good handshake. Loose, floppy, "dead fish" handshakes betray weakness. They make the person behind the hand seem submissive. Crushing, jerky handshakes that throw the receiver off balance make the person shaking seem too aggressive, domineering, and generally off-putting. Handshakes that last too long feel too intimate, while handshakes that are too short feel dismissive. To master your first impressions with people, you must first master the art of a handshake.

There are a lot of parallels between The Upper Hand framework and the art of the perfect handshake. Both require a balance of pressure, firmness, and flexibility to be used effectively. We want a firm hold that portrays confidence, but we don't want to squeeze with force. We want the right amount of pressure for the right amount of time. We want to hold, but not squeeze.

This final Upper Hand practice is for finding the perfect balance of pressure during an interaction, one that extends beyond the initial handshake. It's aptly called "Hold, Don't Squeeze." Hold, Don't Squeeze is a practice for guiding interactions toward desired outcomes, ensuring you only apply extra pressure at the right time, for the right reason. You must build up your sense of timing and develop a keen sense for when to hold, when to throw in a bit of pressure, and when to pull away altogether.

Better yet, when you know how to expertly hold without squeezing, you'll have a better sense for when others are trying to squeeze you.

There was a time, believe it or not, when Amazon was nothing more than an online bookstore. The business was hemorrhaging money, and investors were struggling to justify giving money to *any* internet company, much less Amazon.com. But founder Jeff Bezos was undeterred.

In 1999, when hundreds of other internet businesses were

HOLD, DON'T SQUEEZE

collapsing under the pressure of the dot-com bust, Bezos went on the *The Tonight Show with Jay Leno* to promote Amazon.com.[2] Leno grilled Bezos about the confusing business strategy.

"Here's the thing I don't understand," said Leno. "The company is worth billions."

"Yes," said Bezos.

"And every time I pick up the paper, each year it loses more money than it lost the year before."

"Yes," Bezos said again.

"The company has *never* made a profit," Leno said.

"That's right," Bezos said, cracking a smile.

A silence passed between the two while Leno tried to wrap his head around the idea. Bezos held the silence, waiting patiently for Leno to catch up. As if to demonstrate his confusion, Leno reached down into his desk and pulled out an Amazon.com-branded pencil, complete with a globe-shaped pencil topper and some jingly bits. He gestured at it as if to say, "Why this?" and the audience roared with laughter.

"Now, why . . . how does it—why—how does it . . . why?" Leno stammered, demonstrating a sense of confusion only the best late-night TV hosts can master.

"Seems like a new math, doesn't it?" Bezos said.

This interview highlighted much of the skepticism Bezos and Amazon.com faced during the late '90s and early 2000s. The company wouldn't turn a profit until 2001.[3] Still, critics didn't bother Bezos. Despite Leno's attempt to pressure him into an explanation, Bezos held his composure. He wasn't deterred. He knew how to run his business successfully, even though it would take time for others to see the path in front of him.

Leno, on the other hand, tried to apply undue pressure to Bezos.

He tried to squeeze. For most people, probing questions about their business' plummeting profits would likely trigger a full-blown stress response. After all, for most entrepreneurs, their business is tied directly to their safety and security. Defending their vision on national television would cause sweaty palms and foreheads. They might even feel offended or attacked, and take off. The TV host took a risk by squeezing Bezos too tight, but Bezos knew how to withstand the pressure.

Instead of bailing on the interview or even jumping to defend his business, Bezos kept his cool. He laughed at Leno's confusion. He maintained eye contact, open body language, and a sense of calm amusement. He even waited for Leno to ask directly before he explained why the business wasn't worth giving up. He didn't apply pressure back on Leno, but instead maintained a calm, open demeanor, which made him look sympathetic to the audience.

Leno lost The Upper Hand when he squeezed Bezos, despite his more advantageous role in the interaction. At the time, Leno had the comfort of his own stage seat, the support of the audience, and the confidence to undermine his guest. He held a more powerful role as the interviewer. He could've chosen to establish an on-air rapport with Bezos, but instead he positioned himself as an adversary.

Leno didn't see the risk he took when he squeezed Bezos. He lacked the ability (as many of us do) to see the future. He couldn't predict Bezos's success. During a time when the internet was little more than a tool for chatting with strangers and ordering books, Leno couldn't have known this interview would circulate for years, painting him as the fool for placing undue pressure on a man who would become one of the richest people in the world.

Today, most of us know the value of pressure during interactions. We know applying pressure to a situation can cause undue

HOLD, DON'T SQUEEZE

anxiety for everyone involved. Time pressure, financial pressure, and social pressure all risk causing stress responses in people. If we hold a financial meeting with a business associate, we can't begin the meeting by saying, "I want money, Steve, and you're going to give it to me . . . or else." Steve will squirm under the pressure and feel trapped or cornered. Or he'll just get up and walk out. Either way, his critical thought process will stop, and his brain will transfer its energy instead to his fight-or-flight response.

Once Steve's stress response kicks in, he might respond with anger, aggression, or a swift exit from the interaction. And once he leaves, he's not likely to come back. He doesn't care to find out what "or else" means.

While squeezing an interaction too tightly is problematic, a loose, laid-back situation isn't always the right option, either. Too little pressure might not properly motivate action. A meeting to secure funding for a new project needs a little pressure. Otherwise, everyone grows frustrated when that meeting veers off track, stalls out, or runs out of time without a plan.

A key component of The Upper Hand is the perfect level of pressure. But we must be cautious with how we choose to use it, because once we add pressure to a situation, it's difficult to remove. We can't toss out an ominous threat and then backtrack to building rapport—we've already squeezed too hard.

For better or worse, salespeople are notorious for applying undue pressure. You've likely met the car salesperson who tries to send you home in a new car even though you told them you're *just looking today*. You've met the electronics salesperson who, upon seeing you approach him, launches into a speech about the latest television technology. He walks you through the models before you even have the chance to say you're looking for a phone charger, not a TV.

You've undoubtedly answered the cold caller who insists on running through their pitch before they put you on the do-not-call list. They all try to convince you to buy what they're selling, but they only succeed in chasing you off.

This is the kind of pressure that's best avoided. Those salespeople are not pressuring you to make the best decision for yourself—they're pressuring you to raise their commission. They're acting unethically by using you to further themselves, ignoring how the situation affects you. If you choose to add pressure to an interaction, you must ensure it's necessary to help the other person make the right decision overall, not the right decision for you alone.

The right level of pressure requires you to understand whether the other person is ready to give an answer on their own time. You can't shoot for the big "yes" during an influential interaction before you know everyone involved is ready to hear it, understand it, and agree to it. A gentle, adaptive level of pressure throughout an interaction is the only solution that results in long-term, ethical relationships, both in and out of the business world.

Why It Works: A Helping Hand

How do we respond to people in trouble? We offer a hand, whether it's to offer help, show support, or give sympathy. We apply light pressure, as if to say, "I understand, and I'm sorry." When people seem lost, we extend a hand for them to hold, and we guide them forward. If we squeeze a little, it's only for a fraction of a second to emphasize a point or sentiment. We don't hold so tight they can't escape our grasp, nor do we linger long enough to make them uncomfortable.

The Upper Hand works best when it acts as guidance, not

coercion. When using influence, you must guide the other person to the best conclusion without dragging them. People respond best when they feel free to make their own decisions. Ample time, information, and consideration invites thoughtful engagement and ownership into the interaction. By using influence, we guide the thought process toward the most useful information that informs their decision. We don't hide details, twist words, or force decisions—doing so would only set us up to fail.

When people feel pressured into saying yes, they lose the ability to think critically. It doesn't matter if they're considering a business deal, a purchase, or some other kind of agreement. When they feel squeezed, the brain, sensing danger, diverts processing power away from the logical brain center (the prefrontal cortex) and supplies it to centers for emotional responses (the amygdala). People then become more susceptible to manipulative influence—the kind that preys on their emotions—but they're also more likely to regret falling for that influence later.

Interactions that rely on pushy, coercive, or demanding tactics can also backfire by causing psychological reactance. If someone tries to influence you, and you feel your freedom is threatened—freedom to make a choice, take an action, or think critically in your own time—you're more likely to resist influence until the threat is gone.[4] Further, since reactance is widely considered a motivational state, it may encourage you to take the opposite action being suggested. You might start an argument, abruptly storm off, or, in extreme cases, strike out at the threat. Even if you don't escalate the situation, you're likely to form a negative opinion of the person threatening your freedom.

The amount of reactance you feel largely depends on how big the threat feels to your freedom. Small threats, like a spurt of traffic on the way to a meeting, can cause some annoyance. Larger threats, like surprise expenses you can't afford, urgent tasks you can't complete on time, or blocked exits you can't use, are bound to trigger more aggressive or even hostile reactions.

How hard will you fight for your freedom? Imagine you walk into a clothing store and a salesman greets you at the front door. He asks if you need any help, and you say politely that no, you don't need help, you're just browsing. You make to move on, but he stops you and lists off every deal in the store that day. You wait for him to finish, a little annoyed, but then he dives right into the benefits of opening a store credit card. You don't want to be rude... but you also *don't care* about his sales pitch, and now he's limiting your perceived freedom to move around the store unbothered.

When he finally stops talking, you walk briskly to the other side of the store to look around. You find a rack of jackets and start flipping through them, only to see him standing on the other side of the rack.

"Those are half price today," he says with a smile.

You smush the jackets together and move to a wall of jeans. You hardly have time to unfold a pair in your size before you see his shadow creep up next to you.

"Do you want me to hold those up at the counter for you?" he asks.

You shake your head and drop the pants. You head to the shoe department and duck beneath the rows of cubbies. You're safe now, or so you think. But just as you pop your head up to scan for the sneakers, you see his headset bobbing above the cubbies, like a shark's fin cutting through water. You can't see his lips move, but his words trail after you:

HOLD, DON'T SQUEEZE

"All shoes are buy one pair, get one freeeeeeee!"

That's it, you can't take it anymore! You throw down the clothes in your hands and dart for the exit. No matter how good the deal is, it's not worth dealing with the salesclerk. You've felt pressured since you walked in the door, so it's time to *get out*. Except, you're not fast enough. The door is in sight, but so is he. He smiles at you as he slips right into your escape path.

"Did you find everything you were looking for today?"

You must decide: dart around him or crash through him. You bank left and skid on the linoleum floors as you move around him. You almost lose your footing, but you stick the landing and sprint to the doors. You make it through and wipe the sweat off your forehead. It was a close call, but you made it. You're free.

Most of us have experienced a similar situation at least once—although it may not have been so dramatic. Still, the more salespeople bombard us from all angles, the more we feel tracked, trapped, pressured, and sometimes threatened. Our stress response spikes. Our reactance kicks in and we grow more annoyed by the minute. Every time an employee offers to "help" us, we create a new association with the store we're in: *Do Not Enter—trespassers will be prosecuted to the highest extent of today's sale!*

Guiding someone toward a shared goal, rather than squeezing them until they reluctantly agree, promotes thoughtful engagement during interactions. We can avoid triggering "buyer's remorse" by making sure they have all the information they need to make a decision. Then, when they finally do give the official "yes," they feel a sense of ownership over their choice. They're less likely to turn back on their decision, and more likely to let it guide their future decisions, when it feels like a choice made freely.

What might our predatory salesman in the scenario above have done differently? Instead of lurking around corners to pounce on unsuspecting customers, what if he instead acted as a guide?

Rather than starting the conversation by asking if you need help, the salesman comments, pointing to your shirt, that he loves Yosemite National Park too—its logo is on your shirt. He then asks if you need any help. When you tell him you don't, he nods politely and returns to his post, folding a few tees for a display. He waits patiently there, exactly where customers can find him should they decide they *do* need his help. You are free to peruse the shelves at your leisure, so you do! You find a pair of pants you like, but you don't see it in your size. Lucky for you, there's someone up front who can help you with that.

Since you're feeling safer in this scenario, you have no trouble approaching the salesman and asking him where you can find extra sizes.

"Oh, no worries," he starts. "I'll check the back for you, and come find you."

You wander off into the shoe department, and he finds you trying on some sneakers. You don't need new sneakers, but as he hands you the correct-sized pants, he inquires after the ones you picked out.

"What drew you to those shoes?" he asks.

You mention you were thinking you could use a new pair for an upcoming vacation.

"Oh, cool, where're you headed?"

You mention the Grand Canyon and Tucson for the emerging foodie cuisine.

"Sounds amazing," he says. "You'll have to compare views with Yosemite!" He pauses, looking at the shoes you've picked out. "Those

HOLD, DON'T SQUEEZE

sneakers would work with these pants—let me know if you need anything else." He returns to his post.

There is some pressure here, but it's virtually undetectable. He connects with you, affirms your shoe choice, but applies no pressure to buy—he doesn't even mention the buy-one-get-one-free deal on the shoes. The salesman isn't necessarily playing it cool—he's just not applying heavy pressure like so many others do. You're more likely to approach him with any other questions than any other salesperson on the floor, since he successfully helped you once already. His confident smile and competent behavior make him more approachable. Instead of pressuring you to choose to buy from his store, he simply responds to the choices you make as you make them.

By the time you're finished in the store, you've rounded up six items with the help of the salesman. You asked him where to find shirts on sale, and he showed you the best selection in the clearance section. You happily grabbed three tees. When it comes time to check out, he suggests you open the store credit card to receive another 10 percent off your purchase. There's no annual fee, and you can cancel it at any time. The salesman looks at you with a kind, reassuring smile. You agree.

In this new scenario, the salesman's simple, low-pressure guidance allowed him to hold greater influence when it came time to make the big ask—having you sign up for the store credit card. Rather than acting like a human pop-up ad, he took on the role of a gentle guide. He was ready to help if needed, but unwilling to seem desperate for a deal. He allowed you freedom to make your own decisions over the items you bought, which made you more likely to buy. By holding off on aggressive influence tactics, he managed to meet his goal.

That is the power of the Hold, Don't Squeeze practice.

How to Hold, Not Squeeze

Mastering this practice is like mastering any handshake, helping-hand gesture, or perfect hug. It's all about creating the three C's: comfort, confidence, and competence. As any interaction goes on, maintaining a balance of pressure and leeway sets you up best for success.

Mastering this practice relies on active listening, empathy, and trustworthiness. Once you've got a firm grip on those social skills, you're well prepared to adapt your influence strategy in real time, adjusting pressure levels to ensure the perfect interaction.

Let's examine how to execute the Hold, Don't Squeeze practice through an interaction between a journalist and the person they're interviewing. The journalist, Sarah, must convince her subject, Bob, to give as much information as possible for her hard-hitting story about the mistreatment of low-level employees at the company where he works. There's a lot at stake in this interaction. Bob wants to tell the truth without losing his job, and Sarah wants to expose the company without putting herself, her news site, or Bob at risk.

Sarah's first move is to make Bob as comfortable as possible to speak with her. A comfortable level of pressure during an interaction can motivate the other person to make a decision or provide information freely, without force or coercion. Sarah chooses a public yet intimate space to meet with Bob—a local coworking space—that's comfortable enough to motivate open information sharing. She rents out a private room with glass walls, ensuring their conversation is private but not restricted. She even chooses the seat farthest from the door so Bob feels safe to leave the conversation at any point.

Once the two are seated, Sarah begins the interview by letting Bob know she's aware of the risk he's taking. She thanks him for

HOLD, DON'T SQUEEZE

choosing to trust her, and she promises not to use his name in her report. She reminds him he is free to step out or leave altogether whenever he wants. Then, to ensure total comfort, she asks him outright if there's anything else she can do to make him feel more comfortable.

"Is there anything I can get you? Water, tea?" she asks. "I have snack chips here too."

"A glass of water would be nice," Bob says.

"No problem," says Sarah, who pours him a glass.

By addressing the things that were already increasing this interaction's pressure, Sarah shows effort in making Bob comfortable. Her setup limits Bob's reactance by making him feel free to choose his engagement level. They start off stronger thanks to her effort.

Sarah must keep showing signs that she is on Bob's side. She must recognize his pain point and reassure him that by accepting an interview with her, he is making progress in alleviating that pain. She must also convince him that she's invested in his progress. She's aligned with his goal. She wants to help him, but he must help her too.

Sarah can't convince Bob she is competent enough to help him if she's not confident in her abilities. She can display confidence by setting strong expectations for their meeting. She demonstrates her experience interviewing others by anticipating Bob's needs, and addressing common concerns before Bob even recognizes them. She knows her position as the person with The Upper Hand, and she uses it respectfully.

"I have a tape recorder here," she says, pointing to a device on the table, "but it's just a quick way for me to keep notes while keeping my full attention on you. The recording itself will never leave my possession. No one but me will hear your voice. Is that okay with you?"

"Yes, that's fine," says Bob.

THE UPPER HAND

Having received permission, Sarah flicks on the recorder.

Now, Sarah has addressed Bob's physical discomfort. The next step is for her to approach Bob with empathy, increasing her perceived trustworthiness and encouraging him to feel comfortable with her.

"I reached out to you for this interview because you're one of the dockworkers for FishCo," Sarah says, "and it's my understanding that you've experienced the unsafe working conditions that FishCo claims their employees don't go through."

"Yes, that's right," Bob says. "They don't give us the right tools for the job. The boxes we unload from FishCo ships are heavy, but they don't give us back braces. The carts we need to move stuff from the boats are all broken, and they don't replace them for us. We have to move it all by hand."

"That must be really hard for you," says Sarah. "Have you had a lot of back pain as a result?"

"Yes, ma'am," says Bob.

"Tell me more about your day-to-day life at FishCo's docks," Sarah says.

Throughout the interview, Sarah lets Bob set the pace. She asks open-ended questions and allows him to speak at his leisure. She offers breaks, keeps his water glass full, and waits patiently when he shows signs of resistance. She uses mutual self-disclosure, revealing relevant personal details about herself as a display of trust in Bob, which has the effect of making Bob feel it is safe to share as well. And when Bob struggles to make his point, she does not push back—she displays confidence in herself and in Bob.

Her last consideration is to present competence. Sarah wants Bob to know she is confident in her own abilities, but confidence alone doesn't equal competence. She could be the world's most confident

HOLD, DON'T SQUEEZE

journalist for no reason other than her own ego. If she wants to earn higher levels of cooperation, she must show Bob that she's the right journalist for the job.

Sarah accomplishes this by asking the right questions. She did her research on FishCo before reaching out to Bob for the interview. When he's finished answering her open-ended questions, she follows up with questions that guide him toward the answers she needs most.

"So, you mentioned your back pain earlier," she says, "I've spoken with a few other employees who share your pain. They had trouble finding medical care for their issues since FishCo doesn't provide health insurance to their dockworkers. Can you tell me more about your own experience? Did you tell your boss about your pain? Did you seek help from a doctor?"

"Yes, I told him, but he told me not to see a doctor because I'd get fired," said Bob. "He said FishCo doesn't do worker's compensation."

"That sounds like a tough situation," Sarah replied. "Can you tell me the name of the person who told you this?"

Here, Bob hesitates. He struggles to answer the question because he's worried doing so will come back to haunt him. He doesn't want to lose his job, and revealing his boss's name narrows down the potential "snitch" on his team.

If Sarah wants the answer to her question, she's going to need a little added pressure. She doesn't need to squeeze the information out of Bob—doing so would only make him more stressed. Instead, she can guide him toward the right decision by reminding him of the stakes and their shared goal.

"I know this is hard for you," Sarah says, seeing his concern, "and you don't have to answer any questions that make you uncomfortable. If you don't want me to name your boss, I won't. I just want you to know that if we don't hold these people accountable for their actions, it's going to be hard to make any real change. It's easy to deny accusations if there aren't credible stories to support them. Attaching a name makes it credible, traceable."

"Okay," Bob says, "I understand. I'll give you his name. But you're not going to use mine, right?"

"Right," Sarah says, smiling.

By the end of the interview, Sarah gains all the information she needs to write the perfect exposé on FishCo's work environment. She kept Bob comfortable enough to elicit the right information from him. She showed confidence and competence, which made him trust her with his story. She maintained the right amount of pressure—even though it changed over the course of the interview—to keep Bob talking without making him feel cornered. Together, Bob and Sarah took the best possible steps to achieve their goals through collaboration.

Approaching interactions with the intention to set a shared goal, maintain high levels of comfort, and form long-lasting relationships primes you for better pressure management. Your goals prevent you from exerting undue pressure on people when they don't immediately give you the results you need.

How do you determine how much pressure to apply to an interaction? You start by learning as much as you can about the person you want to influence. What kind of pressure can they handle without feeling offended, coerced, or threatened? Ask plenty of open-ended questions. You can ask about similar experiences they've had in the past—what worked out well? What didn't? If they answer, "I felt scammed," that might be a signal to take the interaction slow so you can build up trust. However, they might say, "The last guy strung me along for six months!" That's your cue to take a more straightforward approach when you make the big ask.

You can also avoid undue pressure by giving transparent answers to the questions you're asked. Open, honest answers that directly address concerns and provide crucial information build trust. An authentic question-and-answer session is a key component of any influential interaction, and when it's done well, it gives everyone what they need to feel confident and capable to say yes.

Some people will need more than one interaction to influence. This is especially true if your first interaction is also your first time meeting them. Since people build trust in you by seeing consistent, competent results, they may need more time to familiarize themselves with you. Recognizing that the first meeting doesn't always result in an official agreement helps remove some of the pressure on you and your interaction partner.

Dumping information on another person in an interaction can add unintentional pressure, so spreading out information over time can be helpful. Humans' short-term memories can hold a finite amount of information, which limits the amount of progress we can make during a single interaction.[5] Big projects or agreements are more difficult to detail, and they make it harder for the person agreeing to keep all the terms at the front of their minds. Once their working memory is full, any additional information will only overwhelm them.

Similarly, you can prevent yourself from feeling overloaded with information by doing research ahead of time. Preparation allows you to be more considerate in your answers and questions. It can aid in adapting lines of questioning during an interaction. At first, it might seem difficult to hold a bunch of knowledge about a person or company as you attempt to influence them, but, like any skill, with practice it becomes easier to see where to head during an interaction.

Ample time for processing is equally beneficial for the influencer. The more prepared you are before you attempt to influence someone, the more likely you are to learn new information. Giving yourself time to process how any new information affects your influence strategy will make it even stronger. It takes a master influencer to adjust an influence strategy moment by moment.

Account for this slow-burning influence by planning ahead. If you need to secure a simple "yes" by Friday, you'd better start the influence process on Monday, not Thursday. If the other person feels like there isn't enough time to properly assess the situation, they may feel the pressure isn't worth the potential reward. Providing ample time for the other person to think through what they're agreeing to makes them more likely to agree. It also makes you less likely to succumb to unethical practices, making them feel uncomfortable, frustrated, or trapped because of you.

The downside to a slower, multiple-interaction approach is that you run the risk of losing the other person's attention. You can mitigate this risk by securing smaller "yeses" that build up to a bigger, final "yes." For example, during the first interaction, you can gain a small "yes" by simply collecting contact information. This opens the door for scheduling future meetings. During the next few meetings, you can assign small, easy tasks for them to complete to keep the momentum up. Have them read an article that relates to your shared goal. Give them a thought prompt to revisit between meetings. By asking them to invest time between interactions, you retain their attention and make them more familiar with your overall goal.

It's difficult to prescribe a formula to know the right moment to squeeze *just enough* for a final "yes." Every situation is different.

HOLD, DON'T SQUEEZE

Sometimes there is a bit of time pressure that makes the slow game impossible. Some situations are dire enough to exclude signs of enthusiasm (like planning a funeral or transitioning out of a relationship). There is no clear-cut sign to determine when a person is perfectly primed to finish a deal. It would be great if the human brain triggered a nonverbal response that signaled that we're in the endgame. It would be amazing if someone scratched their head and rubbed their tummy as an unconscious sign of susceptibility, but alas, we're simply not wired that way.

Instead of searching for an elusive sign that someone is ready to collaborate, it's a more reliable approach to gauge how balanced an interaction feels as it goes on. If the pressure feels too high—if you feel your stress response bubbling up or see signs of the same in the other person—it's a good time to relieve some of the pressure with a break, a digression, or another slight adjustment. If you feel frustrated by a slow, unyielding conversation, you can turn up the pressure a little at a time, like you're trying to find the perfect shower temperature without burning yourself. Keep comfort, confidence, and competence at the forefront while you interact with others, and you're more likely to see signs to raise or lower the pressure.

When to Let Go

Influence is powerful, but it's not magic. There is no guarantee that even a perfectly executed influence strategy will succeed. In some situations, you're bound to recognize there is no happy ending for everyone involved. These are the cases in which you must decide the right moment to let go.

Holding on too tightly to someone who wants to leave an

interaction is almost guaranteed to ruin your influence. You'll trigger their stress response, which will cause them to wrench themselves free of you, and you'll lose any leverage you've gained. If you recognize the other person isn't ready to give a final answer, it's best to let go, rather than forcing them to turn a potential "yes" into a "no" by squeezing too hard.

When your influence plan relies on you securing a final decision, letting go can feel like failing. It can be stressful to think about extending your plan to include extra interactions and longer sustained influence. This is especially true if you're facing a deadline, or you're expected to defend the delay to other people. When this stress strikes, it's tempting to shift tactics and deliver an ultimatum to the person you're trying to influence. At least that way, you might think, you'll have an answer one way or another.

Ultimatums are threats disguised as choices. "If you don't act now, you'll lose this offer" seems like it presents two options: make a decision now or don't. However, there is a hidden threat in there: "say yes, or I'll raise the price, change the terms, or stop negotiating altogether." You slide into the world of unethical influence, since this tactic means making the other person feel like their vulnerabilities are leveraged, forcing them to act outside their own free will. Ultimatums are manipulative, and they're more likely to backfire than a straightforward, "It's time to make a decision."

Forcing an ultimatum on someone is another way to trigger psychological reactance. Presenting an ultimatum is like forcing iron bars to fall from the sky—you trap the other person in a cage and dangle the keys in front of them. This changes the dynamic of the relationship and, in turn, changes the goal of the other person. They stop wanting to work together, and focus instead on how to get their freedom back.

If you do resort to an ultimatum, you lose The Upper Hand. You slide from influence to coercion. Even if the other person accepts your terms, the pressure you've applied will leave both of you in an insecure relationship. You'll both worry that your terms were only accepted out of fear, force, or obligation. Trust will erode. Reaching goals will be harder. And when the deal is done, it's unlikely you'll ever make another.

Instead of squeezing a final answer out of someone, it's much more effective to practice patience. Dismissing time pressure or a frantic need for a definite answer makes the other person feel more comfortable. When they have time to think through their choice, determine trustworthiness, and examine all the pros and cons of an agreement, they'll feel safer and more comfortable, which makes them more likely to agree with enthusiasm.

When you sense an interaction dwindling out without a final decision, *let it go*. Inform the other person you're always available to talk through any questions, comments, or concerns. Schedule a follow-up interaction to continue the influence process on a timetable they're most comfortable using. Leave the door open for them to come back to you instead of locking them inside. Demonstrate trustworthiness by giving them enough room to move in and out of interactions with you freely. It might seem paradoxical, but letting them leave can be the most likely way to ensure they'll come back.

The Upper Hand framework isn't 100 percent guaranteed in any interaction; that's what makes it honest. All influence strategies have the potential to fail because they rely on consistent results from inconsistent creatures. Humans are fickle. Our experiences are unique, our feelings are complex, and our decision-making skills depend on a plethora of underlying factors. The best we can do is utilize our understanding of how the brain works and what drives people to cooperate. That's how we earn success.

Chapter 10

THE PROSOCIAL ENGINEER

Throughout this book, we have explored the techniques of prosocial engineering and influence. From the words we speak to the tone we use, every aspect of our interactions with others can influence them toward our intended outcomes. But there is one more factor that can influence a person's outcomes: the environment in which these interactions take place.

Once you've explored how The Upper Hand promotes successful influence in your own interactions, you might start to notice how the same principles of human behavior shape how people interact in different spaces. Why is it that most people prefer certain paths in a park? Why do grocery stores stock candy in a specific aisle and at the checkout? Why does one friend's house feel inviting while another's manages to inspire dinners out at restaurants? Could a salesperson close more leads than another just based on having a "better" office?

When it comes to design, we may not always be consciously

thinking of how to put others at ease, but there are plenty of professionals, organizations, and companies considering it. Just as a stage sets the scene for a dramatic performance, the physical spaces we inhabit play a vital role in shaping human behavior. From the ambient lighting to the temperature of the air, environmental cues can subtly nudge people toward certain actions and decisions. In the hands of a skilled social engineer, the environment becomes another way to subtly guide a subject to a prosocial outcome.

Make no mistake: social engineering is most powerful through communication—hence the "social" part. That being said, there is one mitigating factor that, while not as strong or dependable as The Upper Hand, can still impact the seamlessness of an interaction. Social engineering is all about influencing others, but it's not always limited to one-on-one or even group interactions. Social engineering is all around us, and once you know what you're looking for, you'll see it in more places than you'd expect.

Social Engineering and the Environment

The modern world is designed through social engineering. The more we learn about how humans interact in the world, the more that knowledge informs environmental factors. Modern architecture, city planning, marketing and advertising, and interior design are all influenced by social engineering.

Social engineering guides how people operate in most spaces. When we understand the core principles of common human behaviors, we can recognize how much social engineering is all around us, attempting to influence our everyday choices. From your favorite amusement park to your go-to convenience store, you experience subtle nudges toward one decision or another everywhere you go.

One of the most famous examples of socially engineered environments exists in the Disney theme parks. In Orlando, the Magic Kingdom's park design puts the customer experience first, going so far as to dig out and create a man-made lagoon that all guests must cross to move from the parking lot to the theme park. Guests are literally transported to a new land via boat or monorail, and that's only the beginning.

Once guests arrive at the Magic Kingdom, the first sight they see is a towering, glittering castle. The pavement is replaced with brick pathways. Scents of fresh popcorn and baked goods are pumped up into the streets through hidden vents. As far as they look, guests will struggle to find any modern technologies to distract them from their fantastical experience. They're inside the magic now, and great pains were taken to ensure they're not removed before they decide to leave.

Magic Kingdom is broken up into five different lands: Main Street USA, Fantasyland, Tomorrowland, Frontierland, and Adventureland. Each is meant to fully envelop its guests, but for this to be effective, the park needed a way to separate them for both guests and employees. It would break immersion to see a Jack Sparrow on Main Street or a colonial woman strolling through the futuristic Tomorrowland.

To stop mismatching employees from breaking immersion, the park designers built a series of underground tunnels called the Utilidors below the park. Employees can arrive at work, put on their costumes, and make their way to their land without seeing a single guest along the way. The tunnels are also perfect hidden passages for trash removal, delivery management, and shortcuts for emergency services. The guests see the fantasy while the Utilidors help with managing the park's reality.

The Magic Kingdom's design hides its modern features for the sake of immersion. For example, each building on the park's main entrance strip, Main Street USA, has an American flag at the top. However, if you look closely, you'll notice none of the flags are real—each one is missing either a star or a stripe. That's because the flags are faux decorations to hide the poles beneath them, which are actually lightning rods, there to protect guests from Florida's surprise summer storms.

The park is also famously efficient, though it hides it well. Main Street USA is built on a slight upward slope so that guests take their time moving toward the castle (and through all the shops) but hustle back down when it's time to leave for the night. In every land, there's a trash can about every 30 paces, which influences guests to toss their trash in the available bins instead of on the ground. These bins have pneumatic chutes under them that suck the trash down into the Utilidors for easy cleanup.

Each Disney park, from Anaheim to Tokyo to Paris, is designed to influence guests to tap into their inner child. By putting the guest experience first, the Walt Disney Company sees larger returns from their guests. Adults are more likely to buy a giant sundae or a Mickey Mouse T-shirt when the world they're in deems it socially acceptable. The Disney theme parks are a testament to modern social engineering, and they're only improving their efforts as the science of influence grows.

You don't have to make the trip to a Disney park to see social engineering at work, though. There is proof of social engineering in your everyday life. Take your local grocery chain, for example: the store is designed to socially engineer a more pleasant—and therefore more lucrative—shopping experience.

Most grocery stores take the principles of The Upper Hand into consideration when designing their store. A grocery store's layout, music, lighting, and even the scents wafting through the aisles are proven influence factors for the average customer.[1] The human drives for safety, connection, and self-identity protection are all accounted for in grocery spaces. The design considers the mind-body feedback loop and makes use of the fact that we, as humans, are our brains.

The layout of a store can influence how safe a customer feels—are the aisles big enough for them to move freely? Are the exits clearly marked and easily accessible? Since the COVID-19 pandemic, many stores increased space between aisles to maintain social distancing. Some of us may not consciously notice these small safety factors, but our brains take note of how safe we are in any given space. The safer we feel, the more we can focus on shopping.

Most grocery stores have spaces designed for communication and connection. Sometimes they're free sample stands, where customers chat and snack with friendly customer service representatives. Other times, stores have entire community gathering areas. They're often coffee shops, bars, or even small food courts within the grocery stores.[2] These seating areas offer customers a place to catch up with neighbors or meet for a drink. Sometimes they double as spaces for demonstrations like cooking classes, seminars, and health fairs. They offer space for customers to stick around, spend more, and come back again.

Grocery stores put a lot of effort into making customers feel comfortable while they shop. We, as influencers, already know how the mind and body affect each other's comfort levels. The grocery store designers know this, too, which is why they put physical and mental comfort on their priority list. They pump warm air in the winter and cool air in the summer to keep the temperatures pleasant. Even the music they play keeps customers moving at a leisurely pace through the aisles.[3] When they slow down, they feel calmer—and they spend more.

Grocery products even go so far as to make their packaging appeal to their customers' self-identity. If you're someone who feels self-conscious about what they put in their cart, you can curb that feeling with packages covered in "All-Natural" and "Organic." Even if the product's nutritional value is no better than the full-fat, extra-processed alternative, it looks healthier. It makes people feel better about their choices when shopping.

All these factors come together to create an experience that encourages spending time, money, and energy inside grocery stores. Smaller techniques like putting "essential" items—milk, bread, and eggs—at the back of the store does the same. Grocery store designers use social engineering to increase their profits, their reputation, and their customer satisfaction.

Even online, social influence determines how likely we are to choose certain businesses, products, and activities. Online reviews help potential customers decide whether to engage with a business. Google reviews and Yelp give broad reviewers a place to share their experiences with others. Some apps and websites have their reviews built right in, like Uber, Airbnb, and Booking.com.

There is a strong, looping connection between humans' biopsychosocial imperatives and our everyday decisions. When we see the connection for what it is—social engineering—we can revolutionize the way we interact with the "real world" around us. We can recognize how it works on us, then make it work for us.

Crafting Lasting Influence

The environmental considerations for social engineering can help you build a space designed for influence. You don't have to be an architect or an interior designer to create rooms that cultivate meaningful interactions. Knowledge about what makes people feel comfortable, confident, and competent can enhance your meeting spaces to influence the people you invite inside. By incorporating your newfound human behavior expertise into your environment, you practice being a prosocial engineer.

You can redesign your office to help you facilitate influence in a business setting. Building a socially engineered office is all about striking balance: you want the space to feel comfortable enough to avoid distraction, but not so comfortable that people see it as a second break room. Soft but bright lighting, one or two armchairs, and a midrange temperature should suffice. You want your office to portray your competence, so it must stay neat and organized. But if it's so neat that it feels sterile, you're likely to hinder your perceived trustworthiness. A few family photos, a framed diploma, and a knickknack or two strike a safe balance. Finally, you pick out a desk chair that's slightly taller than the other seating in the room. It's a small touch, but it makes you feel confident, so it works.

If you're taking a larger business meeting in a public space, your knowledge of influence can still help you choose a place even if you haven't designed it yourself. Restaurants like barbecues or buffets don't bode well for influence—no one wants to talk business when they're covered in sauce, nor when someone leaves the table every 10 minutes. A place with neat, small meal choices is better suited for conversation. You can further encourage everyone's comfort by choosing a restaurant with plenty of food options, like vegetarian, vegan, and dairy-free food, and both alcoholic and nonalcoholic drink options. That way, no one struggles to find their favorite options, and space is freed up to focus on the interaction.

At home, you can even rearrange the places you gather most to influence social interactions. Rooms with semicircle seating promote conversations, while rooms with all furniture huddled around a TV are perfect for group movie nights. Circular dining room tables are best for creating group conversations that feel intimate, while long, rectangular tables tend to cause smaller conversations to crop up at either end. Bright lighting promotes energy, while dimmer settings create a sense of intimacy that can be valuable for private conversations between one or a few people. Whether you're socializing in a family room, dining room, or backyard patio, the design choices you make can help foster a thriving gathering.

As you continue on your journey to master The Upper Hand, you will undoubtedly see your impact on the world around you. On a small scale, you'll see meaningful improvement in your ability to make new connections, business partners, and even friends. The relationships you made before will soar to new heights when you reapproach them from a perspective of mutually beneficial collaboration. Once you make a conscious effort to connect with the people in your life, you may realize how little you actually connected before. You might even learn new things about people you've known for years.

On a larger scale, your mastery of The Upper Hand can encourage better decisions within your team, your company, and your community. The more you strive to make your team feel comfortable, competent, and confident, the more empowered they become. Who knows what new accomplishments they'll earn under your new, ethical, influential approach? Your colleagues and even your bosses may be surprised by the levels of success you achieve once you've got a proven strategy for fostering collaboration.

Outside of the workplace, you may find new interest in influencing parts of your community. You might feel strongly enough to start a petition, influencing your neighbors to band together over a shared cause. You may use your influence for community betterment, organizing litter cleanups, tree-planting groups, or support chains for local families down on their luck. Or perhaps your influence works as simply as encouraging your local coffee shop owner to provide more seating, giving customers more room to hang out, feel comfortable, and buy a second cup of joe.

The influence strategies you use will determine your legacy. Will you go on to be known as one of the most cunning, influential masters of human instinct, like the great Sherlock Holmes? Or will you resort to manipulating, cheating, and playing mind games with your victims, like his nemesis, Professor Moriarty? How you are known among your colleagues and community depends on how you choose to interact with the people around you.

The legacy of a person's impact rests not on fleeting transactions, but on the lasting impressions they create through consistent, positive, connection-rich interactions. When you choose to use your knowledge of influence to help people make better decisions, you create positive change. You instill value and meaning into your relationships. You make people's lives easier, more successful, and better for having met you.

When you consistently use prosocial engineering in your interactions, people won't just join your tribe; they'll seek it out. They won't just speak your language once; they'll learn it long term so they can share a stronger, longer connection to you. They'll know you well enough to see when you're struggling and pants themselves so you don't have to. They'll show you every item on their inner shelves and appreciate every item resting on yours. As you make a habit of reaching out with an open hand, you'll be surprised how often the people in your life will do the same for you.

Humans long for connection. The Upper Hand *is* connection.

However you decide to engage with social engineering and influence, you do so with the knowledge of how powerful these tools are in the right hands. Influence strategies only continue to succeed over time when they're rooted in morally sound principles. Long-term influence requires consistency, trustworthiness, and true connection. The more authentically you engage with others, the more likely you are to be naturally influential.

The Upper Hand has the power to shape our interactions and create positive change in our relationships. Whether we're encouraging better decisions in our community or fostering connections in our own lives, the principles of influence can guide us to the best possible outcomes. Let's continue to navigate the complexity of human interactions with empathy, integrity, and purpose. Let's lead others forward with a gentle, guiding Upper Hand.

Acknowledgments

To my father: Thank you for standing by my side through every challenge, teaching me strength, hard work, and how to hold my ground. You're the first person I want to call, no matter the news—big or small—because I know you'll always be there to listen and support me. I wouldn't be the person I am today if not for you showing me that true strength does not require coldness, and that a warm, loving heart is the strongest thing.

To my sisters, Leigh and Chelsie: The love between us is unwavering. We might argue and say things we regret from time to time (Chelsie, I'm looking at you), but I love you both immensely and wish you all the success in the world. Thank you for never giving up on me.

David Keately, you continue to inspire me every day. I admire you more than I can say, hoping that someday I might possess even a fraction of your intelligence. You believed in me when I couldn't, and you helped me find my footing as a researcher and scientist. I am eternally grateful.

ACKNOWLEDGMENTS

Joe and Thryth Navarro, although we may not be tied by blood, you are my family. I cannot thank you enough for the way you took me into your home and poured love and self-belief into me. I am constantly amazed by the kindness and passion with which you both approach everything and I am continuously inspired by the hard work you put into all you do. I hope to always make you both proud.

Judd, some people come into our lives, and we instantly recognize their lasting significance. You are one of those rare souls. From our very first conversation, I knew you would be a lifelong friend. It fills me with pride to witness your successes, and sharing even a part of this journey with you is an honor. I can't wait to see all that we achieve together.

Dr. Susan, I am profoundly grateful for your guidance. You have taught me so much, and your wisdom is a gift to the world. Thank you for believing in me.

And finally, to you, the reader: Thank you for taking the time to explore this book. I hope the lessons resonate with you and that you remain endlessly curious about the mysteries of human behavior.

Notes

CHAPTER 1

1. "Aetos Capital Commits $50mil to Tian Rui Hotel Corporation." Hotel Business Review: Articles for Hotel Executives, October 14, 2008. https://www.hotelexecutive.com/newswire.
2. Hadnagy, Christopher. "1: A Look into the New World of Social Engineering," in *Social Engineering: The Science of Human Hacking* (John Wiley & Sons, 2018), 7–8.
3. Whittingham, Ken, dir. "The Merger," *The Office*, season 3, episode 8, NBC, 2006.
4. Breuning, Loretta Graziano. *Habits of a Happy Brain: Retrain Your Brain to Boost Your Serotonin, Dopamine, Oxytocin, & Endorphin Levels* (Adams Media, 2015).
5. Rostovtseva, Victoria V., Mikael Puurtinen, Emiliano Méndez Salinas, Ralf F. A. Cox, Antonius G. G. Groothuis, Marina L. Butovskaya, and Franz J. Weissing. "Unravelling the Many Facets of Human Cooperation in an Experimental Study." *Scientific Reports* 13, no. 1 (2023). https://doi.org/10.1038/s41598-023-46944-w.
6. Freeman, Jonathan B., Ryan M. Stolier, Zachary A. Ingbretsen, and Eric A. Hehman. "Amygdala Responsivity to High-Level Social Information from

NOTES

Unseen Faces." *Journal of Neuroscience* 34, no. 32 (2014): 10573–81. https://doi.org/10.1523/jneurosci.5063-13.2014.

CHAPTER 2

1. Maurer, David W. *The Big Con: The Story of the Confidence Man* (Anchor Books, 1999).
2. While it is true that every human brain works in the same basic ways, there are endless opportunities for such a complex organ to diverge from its evolved function. Neurodiversity, psychopathy, and brain damage are all factors that can alter what we consider "typical" brain function. It's unlikely that neurodiversity specifically would impact the basic drives of The Upper Hand (i.e., survival, connection, self-identity, etc.). However, since we currently lack comprehensive studies, we can't say for sure either way. Bearing in mind there may be exceptions, this book will focus on the neurotypical brain.
3. Izquierdo, Ivan, Cristiane R. G. Furini, and Jociane C. Myskiw. "Fear Memory." *Physiological Reviews* 96, no. 2 (April 2016): 695–750. https://doi.org/10.1152/physrev.00018.2015.

CHAPTER 3

1. Eisenberger, Naomi I. "The Neural Bases of Social Pain." *Psychosomatic Medicine* 74, no. 2 (February 2012): 126–35. https://doi.org/10.1097/psy.0b013e3182464dd1.
2. Seifert, Erica J. *The Politics of Authenticity in Presidential Campaigns, 1976–2008* (McFarland & Company, 2012).
3. Feloni, Richard. "Why All 'Shark Tank' Entrepreneurs See a Psychiatrist After Their Pitch." *Business Insider*, November 5, 2015. https://www.businessinsider.com/shark-tank-entrepreneurs-see-psychiatrist-2015-11.
4. McEvoy, Jemima. "Inside the Secretive World of Shark Tank Deals: Who the Real Winners Are." *Forbes*, January 10, 2023. https://www.forbes.com/sites/jemimamcevoy/2023/01/10/inside-the-secretive-world-of-shark-tank-deals-who-the-real-winners-are.

CHAPTER 4

1. "When Did Our Brain Become 'Modern'?" European Synchrotron Radiation Facility, April 8, 2021. https://www.esrf.fr/home/news/general/content-news/general/when-did-our-brain-become-modern.html.

NOTES

2. Harcourt-Smith, W. E., and L. C. Aiello. "Fossils, Feet and the Evolution of Human Bipedal Locomotion." *Journal of Anatomy* 204, no. 5 (May 2004): 403–16. https://doi.org/10.1111/j.0021-8782.2004.00296.x.
3. Raichle, Marcus E., and Debra A. Gusnard. "Appraising the Brain's Energy Budget." *Proceedings of the National Academy of Sciences* 99, no. 16 (July 29, 2002): 10237–39. https://doi.org/10.1073/pnas.172399499.
4. Wright, Andy. "North Korean Officials Had No Idea What Their Hostages Were Signaling in This Photo." Atlas Obscura, November 16, 2016. https://www.atlasobscura.com/articles/north-korean-officials-had-no-idea-what-their-hostages-were-signaling-in-this-photo.
5. Breuning, Loretta Graziano. *Habits of a Happy Brain: Retrain Your Brain to Boost Your Serotonin, Dopamine, Oxytocin, & Endorphin Levels* (Adams Media, 2015).
6. Dutton, Donald G., and Arthur P. Aron. "Some Evidence for Heightened Sexual Attraction Under Conditions of High Anxiety." *Journal of Personality and Social Psychology* 30, no. 4 (1974): 510–17. https://doi.org/10.1037/h0037031.
7. Inagaki, Tristen K. and Naomi I. Eisenberger. "Shared Neural Mechanisms Underlying Social Warmth and Physical Warmth." *Psychological Science* 24, no. 11 (November 1, 2013): 2272–80. https://doi.org/10.1177/0956797613492773.

CHAPTER 5

1. Hornick, Chris. "The Evolution of Superior Leadership." HBSC Strategic Services, March 2023. https://www.hbsconsult.com/2023/03/leadership-evolution-the-last-book-of-leadership/.
2. Levine, Mark, Amy Prosser, David Evans, and Stephen Reicher. "Identity and Emergency Intervention: How Social Group Membership and Inclusiveness of Group Boundaries Shape Helping Behavior." *Personality and Social Psychology Bulletin* 31, no. 4 (April, 2005): 443–53. https://doi.org/10.1177/0146167204271651.

CHAPTER 6

1. Christiansen, Roger, dir. "The One Where Rachel's Sister Babysits." *Friends*, season 10, episode 5. NBC, October 30, 2003.
2. Sagone, Elisabetta, and Maria Elvira De Caroli. "Locus of Control and Academic Self-Efficacy in University Students: The Effects of Self-Concepts."

NOTES

   Procedia—Social and Behavioral Sciences 114 (2014): 222–28. https://doi.org/10.1016/j.sbspro.2013.12.689.
3. Kulesza, Wojciech, Dariusz Dolinski, Paula Wicher, and Avia Huisman. "The Conversational Chameleon: An Investigation into the Link Between Dialogue and Verbal Mimicry." *Journal of Language and Social Psychology* 35, no. 5 (July 27, 2016): 515–28. https://doi.org/10.1177/0261927x15601460.
4. Kawamichi, Hiroaki, Kazufumi Yoshihara, Akihiro T. Sasaki, Sho K. Sugawara, Hiroki C. Tanabe, Ryoji Shinohara, Yuka Sugisawa, et al. "Perceiving Active Listening Activates the Reward System and Improves the Impression of Relevant Experiences." *Social Neuroscience* 10, no. 1 (September 4, 2014): 16–26. https://doi.org/10.1080/17470919.2014.954732.

CHAPTER 7

1. Masaviru, M. "Self-Disclosure: Theories and Model Review." *Journal of Culture, Society and Development*, 18 (2016). https://www.researchgate.net/publication/301789757_Self-Disclosure_Theories_and_Model_Review.
2. Tobore, T. O. "Towards a Comprehensive Theory of Love: The Quadruple Theory." *Frontiers in Psychology* 11 (May 2020). https://doi.org/10.3389/fpsyg.2020.00862.
3. Gross, J. J. "Emotion Regulation: Affective, Cognitive, and Social Consequences." *Psychophysiology* 39, no. 3 (2002): 281–91. https://doi.org/10.1017/s0048577201393198.
4. Press, Gil. "AI Stats News: 86% of Consumers Prefer Humans to Chatbots." *Forbes*, December 15, 2019. https://www.forbes.com/sites/gilpress/2019/10/02/ai-stats-news-86-of-consumers-prefer-to-interact-with-a-human-agent-rather-than-a-chatbot/.
5. Aronson, Elliot, Ben Willerman, and Joanne Floyd. "The Effect of a Pratfall on Increasing Interpersonal Attractiveness." *Psychonomic Science* 4, no. 6 (June 1966): 227–28. https://doi.org/10.3758/bf03342263.

CHAPTER 8

1. Hunt, Amanda. "Anger, the Boy and the Fence." *Alpha Home*, September 28, 2020. https://www.alphahome.org/anger-the-boy-and-the-fence.
2. Quervain, Dominique J.-F. de, Urs Fischbacher, Valerie Treyer, Melanie Schellhammer, Ulrich Schnyder, Alfred Buck, and Ernst Fehr. "The Neural

NOTES

Basis of Altruistic Punishment." *Science* 305, no. 5688 (August 2004): 1254–58. https://doi.org/10.1126/science.1100735.

3. Lawrence, Jean. "The Road Rage Root Cause." Brunilda Nazario, ed. *Women's Health Guide*, accessed May 6, 2024. https://www.webmd.com/women/features/root-cause-of-road-rage.
4. Fell, Andy. "7-Year Follow-Up Shows Lasting Cognitive Gains from Meditation." University of California, Davis, April 4, 2018. https://www.ucdavis.edu/news/7-year-follow-shows-lasting-cognitive-gains-meditation.
5. Ortner, Catherine N. M., Sachne J. Kilner, and Philip David Zelazo. "Mindfulness Meditation and Reduced Emotional Interference on a Cognitive Task." *Motivation and Emotion* 31, no. 4 (November 2007): 271–83. https://doi.org/10.1007/s11031-007-9076-7.

CHAPTER 9

1. Gould, Skye, and Jenny Chang. "How to Properly Shake Hands in 14 Different Countries." *Business Insider*, March 23, 2018. https://www.businessinsider.com/handshakes-around-the-world-2-2017#united-kingdom-2.
2. McLionHead, Lion. "Jeff Bezos vs Jay Leno in 1999." YouTube Video, July 27, 2018. https://www.youtube.com/watch?v=Pj8CthSn2tI.
3. Hopkins, Colby, "The History of Amazon and Its Rise to Success." *Michigan Journal of Economics*, May 1, 2023. https://sites.lsa.umich.edu/mje/2023/05/01/the-history-of-amazon-and-its-rise-to-success.
4. Steindl, Christina, Eva Jonas, Sandra Sittenthaler, Eva Traut-Mattausch, and Jeff Greenberg. "Understanding Psychological Reactance." *Zeitschrift für Psychologie* 223, no. 4 (October 2015): 205–14. https://doi.org/10.1027/2151-2604/a000222.
5. Miller, George A., "The Magical Number Seven, Plus or Minus Two: Some Limits on Our Capacity for Processing Information," *Psychological Review* 63, no. 2 (March 1956): 81–97. https://doi.org/10.1037/h0043158.

CHAPTER 10

1. Mantratzis, P., G. Tsiotras, Loukas K. Tsironis, and K. Gotzamani. "Exploring the Impact of Supermarket Store Layout and Atmospheric Elements on Consumer Behavior: A Field Research Study in Greece." *Sage Journals* 6, no. 2 (October 2023). https://journals.sagepub.com/doi/10.1177/2516600X231203492.

NOTES

2. Monteros, Maria. "'The Future Is More Local and It Is More Social': Why Grocers Are Developing Third Spaces in Stores." Modern Retail, October 27, 2022. https://www.modernretail.co/operations/the-future-is-more-local-and-it-is-more-social-why-grocers-are-developing-third-spaces-in-stores.
3. Mufeeth, M. M., and A. N. M. Mubarak. "Effects of Background Music Tempo on the Behavior of Customers: In the Case of Supermarket Business." *Journal of Business Economics* 2, no. 1 (2020): 51–58. http://ir.lib.seu.ac.lk/handle/123456789/5030.

Index

A

active listening, 125, 184
adapting to conversations, 126–131
agency, regaining, 149
Airbnb, 200
alignment, 104–105
Amazon, 174–176
amygdala, 42, 43, 82, 179
Anheuser-Busch, 13
Aristotle, 96
arousal, 88
assumptions, 90
authenticity
    in creating a tribe, 123
    for genuine engagement, 136
    and influence, 60–65
    other's resistance to, 153
    in pantsing yourself, 145–147
    reputation built on, 70
    in speaking their language, 114–116, 120
awareness
    of manipulation, 48–49
    self-, 22–23, 155

B

balance
    between compliments and connection, 107–109
    emotional, 167–168
    of pressure, firmness, and flexibility, 173–174 (*see also* Hold, Don't Squeeze)
the beer question, 61
behavior
    bias-dictated, 90
    changing, 81
beliefs
    in building self-identity, 118–119
    building "shop talk" around, 111–112
    causing rifts in interactions, 152
    challenges to, 119–120
    and sense of self, 90
    shared, 92, 96, 117
    shelving your, 160
Bezos, 174–176
biases, 81
    causing rifts in interactions, 152
    confirmation, 117–118

INDEX

biases *(continued)*
    interactions acting on, 90
    that impact others' worldviews, 117
biopsychosocial approach, 73–78
    brain in, 80–82
    connection and collaboration in, 84–86
    and decision making, 200
    drive to survive in, 82–84
    to influence, 4
    mind-body feedback loop in, 87–89
    psychological drives in, 79–80
    self-identity in, 90–92
blame, taking on, 137, 148
body language
    closed, 126
    open, 125–126
    when pantsing yourself, 148
bonds
    building, 107–109
    initial, 98–100
Booking.com, 13, 200
"The Boy with the Temper," 154
brain, 80–81
    and biases, 90
    and challenges to beliefs, 119–120
    and cognitive dissonance, 91
    distinguishing inauthenticity in, 60
    information processing in, 79, 82
    learning by, 59
    mind-body feedback loop in, 87–89
    neural pathways concerning warmth in, 89
    psychological drives processed in, 79–80
    reward system of, 26, 43–44, 85, 86
    split-second judgments by, 27
    survival wiring of, 26, 79, 82–83, 116–117
    when pressured, 179
    wiring for connection in, 85
brand identities, 91
Brown, Brené, 138
buyer's remorse, 59, 68, 181

C

Cadell, Ava, 158
Calvin Klein, 62
capability, in building self-identity, 118–119
China, 12–17, 24
closed body language, 126
cognition, embodied, 88–89
cognitive dissonance, 91
cognitive functions, 81, 117
cognitive relief, self-disclosure as, 144
cognitive shortcuts, 81
collaboration
    assessing readiness for, 191
    and conflicting beliefs, values, or goals, 120
    drive for, 84–86
    human wiring for, 4
    and identity, 119
    intentions for, 59–60
    making room for, 138
    mindset for, 65
    obstacles to, 159
    prosocial engineering for, 21
    strategy for, 53
    strengthened desire for, 117
combative environments, 67–68
comfort
    of commonalities, 116–120
    in creating a tribe, 100–101
    in decreasing resistance, 153
    in design of environments, 201–202
    in grocery store design, 199–200
    in holding, not squeezing, 184–188
    with points of contention gone, 159
    speaking their language for, 111
    (*see also* Speak Their Language)
commonalities
    comfort of, 116–120 (*see also* Speak Their Language)
    connecting over, 97–101 (*see also* Create a Tribe)
    investigating, 121–124
    leaving more room for, 159–160
    (*see also* Shelve It)
communication
    authenticity in, 114–116
    in grocery store design, 199

INDEX

openness of, 152
power in, 114 (*see also* Speak Their Language)
in social engineering, 196
verbal and nonverbal, 113, 114 (*see also* nonverbal communication)
community
    crafting sense of, 98–99 (*see also* Create a Tribe)
    grocery store design for, 199
compassion, 118–119
competence
    in creating a tribe, 100–101
    in decreasing resistance, 153
    in design of environments, 201
    in holding, not squeezing, 184–188
compliments
    in creating a tribe, 104, 105, 107–109
    that create discomfort, 77
computers, structure of, 80
concessions, 40–41
confidence
    in creating a tribe, 100–101
    in decreasing resistance, 153
    in design of environments, 201
    in holding, not squeezing, 184–186, 188
confirmation bias, 117–118
conflicting information, 117–118
connection(s), 2
    authentic, 60–65
    and conflicting beliefs, values, or goals, 120
    in creating a tribe, 105
    establishing, 4
    in grocery store design, 199
    and identity as part of in-group, 120
    inspiring, 97
    mutual, using, 37–38
    over commonalities, 97–101
    with strangers, 23
    through compliments, 107–109
    through speaking their language, 114, 117, 124 (*see also* Speak Their Language)
    in the Upper Hand, 84–86
    Upper Hand as, 204

control
    allowing others to regain, 140–141
    in building self-identity, 118–119
    in manipulation, 3–4
    over emotions, regaining, 140–141, 144–145
    progression of, 37–41
    self-, 155–157
cooperation, 1
    among humans, 26–27
    in creating a tribe, 95, 101
    empowering innate desire for, 49
    handshakes signaling willingness for, 173
    and neural reward networks, 44
    research on, 27–29
    self-identity influencing, 91
    in speaking another's language, 120
    and survival, 26
    in the Upper Hand, 84–86
corporate cults, 39–40
cortisol, 26, 67, 165
Create a Tribe, 95–109
    authenticity in, 123
    building bonds with, 107–109
    strategies for, 103–107
    in Super 8 example, 14
    Upper Hand principles in, 100–103
    variations of, 104–107
creativity, 118–119
critical thinking
    energy used by, 81
    new brain's responsibility for, 79
    suppressing, 42–43
    when pressured, 179
crocodile brain, 79
cult leaders, 43

D

decision making
    biopsychosocial imperatives in, 200
    brain's role in, 81
    cognitive dissonance in, 91
    guiding, not coercing, 179–183
    and physical states, 88–89
    social engineering of, 196–200
    and survival drive, 83
    ultimatums for, 192–193

INDEX

designing environments, 195–200
The Dictator Game, 28–29
dictatorships, 96
Disney theme parks, 140–144, 197–198
distress
    acknowledging your, 165
    from conflicting information, 117–118
The Doctor Is In (podcast series), 2
domineering leadership, 96
dopamine, 58–59
Dragons' Den (TV show), 66
drives, 81
    for connection and collaboration, 84–86
    and design of grocery spaces, 199
    to preserve self-identity, 90–92
    psychological, 79–80
    for survival, 82–84

E

Edelman, 13
embodied cognition, 88–89
emotional cues, 87, 88
emotional discipline, 154–159, 162
emotional intelligence, 154–159, 168
emotional regulation
    inner aspects of, 165–167
    outer aspects of, 165, 167–168
emotions
    brain's processing of, 79, 88
    causing rifts in interactions, 152
    controlling responses to, 155–156 (*see also* Shelve It)
    exposing your, 136–138 (*see also* Pants Yourself; vulnerability)
    of others, context of, 137
    reducing spikes in, 156
    regaining control over, 140–141, 144–145
    self-awareness of, 155
empathy
    in controlling reactivity, 162–163, 165
    in holding, not squeezing, 184
    and manipulation, 46
    from others, earning, 142
    in speaking their language, 131
    sympathy vs., 146–147

energy, for the brain, 81
engagement, genuine, 136
English football fan tribes, 101–103
environments
    combative, 67–68
    comfortable, 89
    designed for influence, 201–202
    safe, 100
    social engineering of, 195–200
    that promote success, 68–69
    for virtual interview, 113
ethics
    conflicting, 120
    disregard for, 78
    and high-pressure tactics, 65–69
    and reputation, 70
    in Upper Hand, 2, 31
    in using influence, 19, 51–57, 69
evolutionary psychology, 60
exclusivity, creating, 104–106
executive functioning, 79, 81
exiting interactions, 137–138
exploitation
    other options instead of, 17
    using social engineering for, 34–37

F

failure
    forgiving, 61
    potential for, 193
familiarity, 103
    for psychological safety, 118
    through speaking someone's language, 118
    and willingness to cooperate, 27–29
fear
    in dictatorships, 96
    reducing, 139–140 (*see also* Pants Yourself)
fear learning (fear memory), 47–48
fight-flight-freeze response, 82, 91, 116–117, 156
Fink, William, 34–36
force, 11, 12, 192–193
freedom, feeling threat to, 179–181
Friends (TV show), 115

INDEX

G
gaslighting, 46
gender bias, 90
goals
    building "shop talk" around, 111–112
    conflicting, 120
    shared, 103, 188
Google, 200
grocery stores, social engineering in, 198–200
guidance, coercion vs., 179–183. *see also* Hold, Don't Squeeze
gut feelings, 73–78

H
habits, changing, 81
Hadnagy, Chris, 2–5, 17, 19
handshakes, 173–174
high-pressure tactics, 48, 65–69
histories, shared, 117
Hold, Don't Squeeze, 173–193
    as guidance, 178–183
    strategies for, 184–191
    in Super 8 example, 15–16
    when to let go, 191–193
honesty, 61, 138
humility, 139
hypothalamus, 82

I
ICAC (Internet Crimes Against Children Task Force Program), 4–7
identity
    attacks on, 90–91
    as part of same in-group, 120
    self-, 46 (*see also* self-identity)
    shared, 106
ideological leaders, 96
immersive customer experience, 197–198
influence, 51–70
    and authenticity, 60–65
    biopsychosocial approach to, 4
    conventional techniques for, 73–78
    deconstructing myth of, 17–24
    defining, 1, 18–19

    designing environments for, 201–202
    by dictators, 96
    and high-pressure tactics, 65–69
    for long-term success, 61, 65
    malicious, 47–49
    and manipulation, 1, 3–4 (*see also* manipulation)
    with mastery of Upper Hand, 202–203 (*see also specific topics*)
    misconceptions about, 54
    power of, 5–6, 8
    prosocial, 53–54
    and reputation, 69–70
    resistance to, 30, 32
    short-term strategies for, 54–60
    trust as core/foundation of, 3, 24–30, 65
    unethical use of, 51–57, 69
    without appealing to identity, 119
information
    avoiding overload of, 189–190
    conflicting, 117–118
    elicited with social engineering, 19–20
    holding back, 151 (*see also* Shelve It)
    in interactions, 30–31
    investigating, validating, and relating to, 121–124
    sensitive, influencing others to give up, 22
    silence in eliciting, 168
    from strangers, 23
information processing
    allowing time for, 190
    in the brain, 79, 82, 87
    energy needed for, 81
    by the unconscious mind, 77
in-groups, 117, 118, 120
insults, shelving reactions to, 160–161
intelligence, emotional, 154–159, 168
intentions, 20, 24, 33–34, 59
interactions
    biases created through, 90
    biopsychosocial analysis of, 78
    course-correcting, 133
    different languages used in, 116

INDEX

interactions *(continued)*
    exerting control over, 136–137
    gracefully exiting, 137–138
    importance of, 7
    intentions in, 59
    letting go of, 191–193
    prosocial approach to, 21–22
    as prosocial games, 30–32
    role of oxytocin in, 27
    as starting point for connections and relationships, 4
    strong resistance in, 152 *(see also* Shelve It)
Internet Crimes Against Children Task Force Program (ICAC), 4–7
investigating, in speaking someone's language, 121, 129–131

J

job applications, 116
Johnson & Johnson, 13
judgments, 90

K

Kayak, 13

L

lasting impact, 201–204
leadership, 95–96
learning
    by the brain, 59
    fear, 47–48
Leno, Jay, 175–176
letting go of interactions, 191–193
leverage, 11–12, 17, 25
Lion's Den Finland (TV show), 66
listening, active, 126, 184
Liverpool Football Club, 103–104
logic, new brain's responsibility for, 79
loyalty, 118–119

M

Madoff, Bernie, 37–38
Magic Kingdom, 197–198
malicious influence, 47–49
Manchester United, 103–104
manipulation
    growing awareness of, 48–49

    influence vs., 1
    as influence without trust, 3–4, 25
    as progression of control, 37–41
    psychology of, 41–47
    and reputation, 69–70
    trust as first step in, 37
Mars Inc., 13
meditation, 162–164
memory, fear, 47–48
middle brain, 79
mimicry, 125
mind-body feedback loop, 87–89, 199
mindful meditation, 162–164
mindfulness
    in controlling reactivity, 162–165
    in self-disclosure, 145–147
mindset
    long- vs. short-term, 65
    of "them vs. me," 67
mistakes
    correcting, 126–131
    destigmatizing, 149
    in shelving reactions, 168–170
morals
    different languages of, 117
    and sense of self, 90
    shelving your, 160
mutual connections, 37–38
mutual consent, 61–62, 70
mutually beneficial interactions, 31
mutual self-disclosure, 138–145

N

Navarro, Joe, 3
neocortex, 79
neural network, computers inspired by, 80
neural pathways, 81
neural reward networks, 43–44
new brain, 79
New York City, 58
New York Fashion Week, 62
Nike, 62
nonverbal communication, 113, 114
    open and closed body language, 125–126
    when pantsing yourself, 148
Northampton University, 112–114

INDEX

O

obstacles to work, 151–152. *see also* Shelve It
OFC (orbitofrontal cortex), 43
The Office (TV show), 25
online social influence, 200
open body language, 125–126
openness, 60–61
    in communication, 152
    reputation built on, 70
orbitofrontal cortex (OFC), 43
oxytocin, 26–27, 86, 99, 173

P

Pants Yourself, 133–149
    authenticity in, 145–147
    as mutual self-disclosure, 138–145
    pantsing others vs., 137
    strategies for, 147–149
    in Super 8 example, 15
Parks and Recreation (TV show), 133–138
patience
    instead of ultimatums, 193
    from others, earning, 142
perceived social groups, 102–103
perceptions, in building self-identity, 118–119
personalization, 27–29
physical appearance, compliments on, 77–78
physical cues, 87–88
physical states, decision making and, 88–89
physical warmth, social warmth and, 89
power dynamics, 12, 25
    in client relationships, 64
    consensual, trust in, 61
    old-school, 95
praise, 77
prefrontal cortex, 179
Presnick, Mitchell, 12–17, 24, 30, 162–163
pressure
    balance of, 174 (*see also* Hold, Don't Squeeze)
    types of, 177
Procter & Gamble, 13
progression of control, 37–41
prosocial engineering, 195–204
    crafting lasting influence with, 201–204
    defining, 20–21
    designing environments, 195–200
    and ethics, 31–32
    in Upper Hand, 21–23, 31–32
prosocial game(s)
    in research on cooperation, 27–29
    Upper Hand as, 30–32
prosocial influence, 53–54
psychics, 42–43
psychological changes, with conventional influence techniques, 76–77
psychological distress, from conflicting information, 117–118
psychological drives, 79–80. *see also* drives
psychological reactance, 179–181, 192
psychological safety, 118
psychology
    evolutionary, 60
    of manipulation, 41–47
    to understand others, 21

R

referrals, 37–39, 52–53
reflecting other's beliefs, values, goals, 111–112
regretful business decisions, 67–68
relating, in speaking someone's language, 121, 123, 124, 129–131
relationships
    establishing, 97 (*see also* Create a Tribe)
    lasting, 4
    manipulation in, 44–46
    meaningful, 70
    opportunities from, 7
    power dynamics in, 64
    prosocial engineering in, 20–21
reliability, reputation built on, 70
reptilian brain, 79
reputation
    building positive, 6
    and influence, 69–70
resistance
    expectation of, 30

INDEX

resistance *(continued)*
    in interactions, 152–153, 163–164
        (*see also* Shelve It)
    to using influence, 32
risk-reward patterns, 30
road rage, 157–158
Ryan, James, 34–36

S

safety, 86
    in creating a tribe, 100
    in grocery store design, 199
    with points of contention gone, 159
    psychological, 118
seating, 202
self
    main components of, 118–119
    self-identity vs., 118
self-awareness
    in emotional intelligence, 155
    and influence tactics, 22–23
self-control, in emotional intelligence, 155–157
self-disclosure
    mindful, 145–147
    mutual, 138–145
self-identity
    allowing others to maintain, 140
    in grocery store design, 199, 200
    instinct to preserve, 160
    investigating others', 122, 124
    losing, in manipulative relationships, 46
    self vs., 118
    as Upper Hand principle, 90–92
    validating, 118
self-regulation, in emotional intelligence, 155, 156
self-trust, 166
senses, triggers of, 76
shame, 44–45
shared interests, 97–100, 104–107. *see also* commonalities
Shark Tank (TV show), 65–69
Shelve It, 151–171
    benefits of, 159–162
    choosing when to react, 168–171
    as emotional discipline, 154–159
    inner responses in, 165–167
    outer responses in, 165, 167–168
    strategies for, 162–168
    in Super 8 example, 163
short-term influence
    and reputation, 69–70
    for single-serve interactions, 57–60
    that sidesteps openness, trust, or authenticity, 60–61, 65
    unsuccessful, 54–57
silence, 168
Simpson, Jay, 61–65, 70
small-scale influence, 5–6, 24
The Social Engineer (podcast), 2
social engineering, 33–49
    defining, 19
    in the environment, 196–200
    for exploitation, 34–37
    and progression of control, 37–41
    and psychology of manipulation, 41–47
    resistance to using, 32
    understanding malicious influence, 47–49
    and Upper Hand, 17–24
Social-Engineer LLC, 17–18, 22, 23
social groups, perceived, 102–103
social safety, 86
social skills, brain signals for, 79
social warmth, physical warmth and, 89
Speak Their Language, 111–131
    adapting to the conversation, 126–131
    authenticity in, 114–116, 120
    comfort of commonalities, 116–120
    strategies for, 121–126
    in Super 8 example, 14–15
squeezing, in interactions, 174–177. *see also* Hold, Don't Squeeze
stereotypes, 90
strangers, getting information from, 23
stress
    psychological reactance to, 179–181 (*see also* Hold, Don't Squeeze)
    reducing, 139–140 (*see also* Pants Yourself)
    socially engineered, 67–68

INDEX

speaking their language to inhibit, 114 (*see also* Speak Their Language)
with the unfamiliar, 103
when identity is attacked, 90–91
stress hormones, 82
success
  earning, 193
  environments promoting, 68–69
  and identity as part of in-group, 120
  long-term, 61, 65
  mutual desire for, 70
  short-term, 54–57
Super 8, 13–17, 24, 30, 163
survival
  brain wiring for, 26, 79, 82–83, 116–117
  and connection, 85, 86
  and cooperation, 26
  drive for, 82–84
  in old-school leadership, 95–96

T

Target, 62
team, building. *see* Create a Tribe
tension, reducing, 139. *see also* Pants Yourself
"them vs. me" mentality, 67
thoughts, mastering your, 164. *see also* critical thinking
three Cs
  in creating a tribe, 100–101
  in decreasing resistance, 153
  in designing environments, 201
  in holding, not squeezing, 184–188
thumbs, 80–81
transparency. *see also* Pants Yourself
  in answering questions, 189
  for genuine engagement, 136
  prioritizing, 70
  as self-disclosure, 139
tribe, connecting to, 85. *see also* Create a Tribe
trust, 1, 27
  borrowed, 37–38
  broken, 36, 46, 48, 59
  building, 189
  in building cooperation, 30

as core/foundation of influence, 3, 24–30, 65
in creating a tribe, 95
handshakes signaling, 173
in holding, not squeezing, 184–186
influence without, 3–4, 25
inspired by authenticity, 61–64
and intentions, 33–34
interactions that sidestep, 60–61
mutual display of, 144
in the professional world, 61–63
proving you are worthy of, 136
reputation built on, 70
self-, 166
self-disclosure for, 143–144
through personal connections, 107
in Upper Hand, 36–37
and vulnerability, 138, 139
truth
  drive to preserve self-identity vs., 91
  human craving for, 60

U

Uber, 200
ultimatums, 192–193
unconscious biases, 90
unconscious mind, information processing by, 77
understanding, from others, earning, 142
unity, crafting sense of, 98–100. *see also* Create a Tribe
Upper Hand, 11–32, 73–93
  brains in, 80–81
  connection and cooperation in, 84–86
  development of, 1–2
  drive to survive in, 82–84
  as guidance, not coercion, 178–179
  and gut feelings, 73–78
  key principles of, 79–80 (*see also individual principles*)
  mastery of, 202–203
  mind-body feedback loop in, 87–89
  as prosocial game, 30–32
  self-identity in, 90–92
  and social engineering, 17–24

INDEX

Upper Hand *(continued)*
    trust in, 24–30, 36–37
    used by Mitchell Presnick, 12–17
USS *Pueblo*, 84–85

V

validating, in speaking someone's language, 121, 122, 124, 129–131
values
    in building self-identity, 118–119
    building "shop talk" around, 111–112
    conflicting, 120
    different languages of, 117
    and sense of self, 90
    shared, 92, 103
ventral striatum (VS), 43, 44
verbal communication, 113, 114
virtual interviews, 112–114
VS (ventral striatum), 43, 44
vulnerability. *see also* Pants Yourself
    to gain sympathy, 146–147
    for genuine engagement, 136
    guarding vs. revealing, 61–63
    power of, 139

W

Walt Disney World, 140–144
warmth, physical and social, 89
worldviews
    finding similarities between, 131
    resisting urge to challenge, 119
    seeking out what confirms or strengthens, 117–118

Y

Yelp, 200
"yeses," small, 190

Z

zero-sum games, 16

About the Author

Dr. Abbie Maroño is both a scientist and a practitioner in the field of human behavior, recognized by the US Department of State as a top 1% behavior analysis expert. Having completed her PhD in psychology, Abbie became a professor of psychology by the age of 23 and is an active member of several internationally recognized research groups.

Underscoring her recognized expertise, Dr. Abbie has provided specialized behavior analysis training for elite units such as the Internet Crimes Against Children (ICAC) Task Force, inclusive of agents from the US Secret Service, FBI, Department of Homeland Security, and local law enforcement agencies. Dr. Abbie is also an award-winning reviewer, expert advisor, coach, author, and keynote speaker. She regularly contributes to Forbes and Apple News and has been featured on major media outlets, including BBC News, WIRED, Forbes Breaking News, and other international platforms.